Tricking the Devil

WAR-TIME DIARY OF A
TEENAGER DURING
THE HOLOCAUST

Dorla Gundersheimer

VANTAGE PRESS
New York

FIRST EDITION

Copyright © 2004 by Dorla Gundersheimer

Published by Vantage Press, Inc.
419 Park Ave. South, New York, NY 10016

Manufactured in the United States of America
ISBN: 0-533-14778-6

Library of Congress Catalog Card No.: 2003097873

0 9 8 7 6 5 4 3 2 1

To Gert and Christopher, who were always there for me

Contents

Preface

In the mid-1930s, when Adolf Hitler was chancellor of Germany, my mother, my brother and I were more and more restricted by tightening measures of the Nazi regime. Slowly but steadily our situation worsened. At first, these tactics were to drive all German Jews out of the country; later, at the beginning of the Second World War, the threats turned deadly. I remember relatives and friends who insisted that they had never done anything wrong and, for that reason, could not be accused. They counted on a civilized society, and they did not know about the gas chambers. How my family of three preserved our humanity and stayed alive through ten years of Nazi brutality is the subject of the following pages.

I am now approaching my eightieth year. Those who know me have said that my history deserves a wider audience. Young people especially are asking me about my teenage experiences during the Second World War. The early memories of my childhood were written down in the 1950s, when I first confronted the facts of my poisoned past. The effects of thinking back were so destructive to my peace of mind that I abandoned all attempts to write for forty years. Instead, I became a high school teacher with a specialty for teens-at-risk. My many years in secondary schools made me realize that my recollections of the Hitler time could be a source of courage and strength for youngsters who have a difficult time growing up.

Tricking the Devil

1. Hohenschäftlarn

The heavy wooden shutters were still closed, and my room was a large, dark space; only under the balcony door sparkled a first ray of sunlight, and it beckoned me outside. There I could see down the hill to the edge of the forest, where the tall, black trees seemed to me to be full of secrets and surprises. Many times I saw the red fox jumping about and the wild rabbits playing hide-and-seek. Far above the treetops, in the distance, I could make out the silhouette of the Alpine mountain chain. Every season had its own attraction—out there on my lovely balcony: In the fall, one could taste the first snowflakes and look forward to toboggans and skiing; in the winter, one could anticipate a visit from St. Nicholas, who would walk out of the forest every year and make his way slowly up the hill toward our house, a farm house with barns and a hayloft.

The balcony has a special place in my memories of childhood, because so many times our father was out there on his deck chair, reading the morning paper. I didn't know at that time that he was a disabled veteran of World War I. I knew about the long, deep scars on his lower back, but I had not made the connection to the lawn chair, where he spent hours every day. The only thing I saw when I found him on the balcony was the opportunity to beg him for one of his fantastic stories: "The Tale of the Silent King and His Talkative Daughter," left lasting impressions because, explained Father, "You must learn to save your words for a time when you have something important to say. The moral is," he con-

1

tinued, "every person has only one hundred thousand words to use and when they are all gone, it's over." I believed every word of his and shuddered at the thought of his hunting trip in the Siberian wilderness. The throw rug on his chair became the hide of a huge bear, and even our mother became the beautiful maiden he found in a snow cave.

When Father finally ordered me back to my room, I usually heard the sound of the piano next door, where my older brother Gert was practicing his music lesson. This would prompt me to start dancing around my room, faster and faster, until he made a mistake and the melody was interrupted. I do not remember one single incident when I had breakfast, because most of the time I did not want to eat. I was much more interested in the project in the hayloft that required many hours of my time. In a big cardboard box, I had gathered four chicken eggs. I carefully knelt down over them and waited patiently, certain that the lively little yellow brood would hatch out of their shells. To my dismay, somebody would always find me and persuade me to appear at the lunch table, where I would sit in front of my plate full of soup long after everybody had finished their dessert.

Early every morning, our mother was gone on her way to Munich where she had a lot to do. Especially on weekends, when her movie theaters were busier than during the week. She was one of the first women in Munich who drove her own automobile, a convertible. Our chauffeur, who mostly assisted our father, showed the greatest respect for her driving ability. He had an unforgettable phrase to announce her return to the house: "The boss lady just drove her car ass-first into the garage!"

Our mother's return from the city was always a joyous occasion. Aside from presents for us children, she often brought home guests who stayed for a while. Dorothea

Wieck, who had known Lonny well since childhood, spent many vacations with us in the foothills of the Alps. Karl Valentin, the Munich comic, told us about the frogs who gathered by the brook in the garden who gave a quaking concert every morning. Nobody followed his invitation for breakfast at 4:00 A.M. Adalbert von Schlettow, who became famous after he played the traitor "Hagen" in the film *Die Nibelungen*, moved into our little garden house and became a part of the family for several months. He insisted that all of us wear the leather pants he had bought for us. After wearing them, I ended up with a boy's haircut, because the local barber could not be convinced that I was a girl in Lederhosen.

Mother had a special gift to involve the movie-going public of the city. For each premiere of a major film, she invited the leading actors personally in order to introduce them to the audience. The stars always accepted gladly, because the publicity was so important for them. Occasionally, this led to difficulty. Pat and Patachon, the forerunners of Abbott and Costello, could not be left alone in their hotel because they would get stone drunk and become unable to walk on the stage. The entire week of their stay in Munich, they had to be chaperoned, and they responded with impolite behavior, to say the least.

There were times when I had a small part in the introduction of film stars. At the premiere of *The Blue Light* (*Das Blaue Licht*), Luis Trenker was handed a bouquet of flowers by me and when William Dieterle came all the way from Hollywood, he kissed me on the forehead in front of a full house. Once in a while, Gert and I were seated in one of the loges; we saw the first Mickey Mouse cartoons from America. In 1931, I saw the premiere of *Der Kongress Tanzt*, with Lillian Harvey and Willy Fritsch. It was an unforgettable

3

event for me, at age seven, when they danced the Viennese waltzes.

I was too young in 1933, to understand why we had to move to the inner city of Munich. I guessed that it was Father's deteriorating health: later I learned that Mother wanted to spend more time at home with him. We had to give up the house on the hilltop and get used to a rather dark apartment in downtown Munich. The difference between my first school year in the village of Schäftlarn and the private school of the rather strict Sisters Ebermeyer in the city was striking. Even though we moved again about a year later to the outskirts of the city, where we had a large park-like garden, I sensed the blow that was to hit us and did not enjoy the new surroundings. It was the last place where our father was still with us; when we had to bury him, the Gestapo was already standing behind us at the cemetery.

2.   The Master Race

The first sign of terror stayed in my mind for a lifetime. My father said, "Hitler is taking over the country and that'll be the end of Germany." I was waiting for my tenth birthday. My big brother had always told me that I would be a little kid until I was ten. "At ten," he explained, "at the age of ten, you become a grown-up." What my brother Gert told me, I always believed. He had taught me to read and write and all kinds of other difficult tasks, and I knew he was right! It turned out that he was this time too: At the age of ten, childhood ended for me.

"Why would it be the end of Germany?" I inquired with the curiosity of a ten-year-old. "Because he will start a war, and he'll lose it, and that will be the end." I was alarmed. Now that I was finally growing up, how could it be the end? I had never seen a big man cry before; I tried to offer comfort: "Can't we do without Germany?" It was all my little girl wisdom could think of. My father seemed huge to me, at least at that time; when I saw him sob like a child, I was deeply shaken. I heard him murmur "I will not survive that," and a sharp pain welled up from my heart into my throat and it stuck there like an indigestible truth that I dared not swallow.

Father was a one hundred percent disabled veteran of the First World War. I remember sneaking into the bathroom behind him one day and seeing two big scars across his back, where something had torn up his right kidney and the base of his right lung. He had met my mother in a field hospital, where she was a volunteer nurse. They married in 1917, and together, they worked in the emerging film industry, managing several movie houses in Munich.

My father's ominous remark about Hitler had an effect on me, because I believed him. When he died two years later, I had carried the burden of his impending death ever since Hitler became the chancellor. Hitler had discontinued all imports in order to save the German economy, and my father's life-saving medicine had come from England. (I believe it was cortisone, but I'm not sure.)

Days after we had buried my father with military honors, my mother heard from the Gestapo, Hitler's secret police organization. As a member of the Jewish race, she found her license to manage movie theaters was cancelled. The disabled veteran of the First World War, with his direct connections to the German army, was no longer in the way of the "Master Race."

My little mother, with enormous restraint, took it calmly and said something to the effect of, "If it isn't one thing, it's another, and I'll have to find a different source of income," but my brother, always the more circumspect, immediately took from it the notion that only a uniform in the family could protect us from such robbery in the future. He was fourteen years old at the time, but his resolve to become the protector of his mother and sister was firm from that time on.

Much of what followed was not made clear to me. With the intent of saving my childhood, "Mutti" (as we called her) and Gert withheld information from me. So much so, that I only sensed something was terribly wrong. I had not the slightest idea at the time what Judaism was. I had grown up in a small village in the foothills of the Alps, south of Munich, and had gone to elementary school with the local farmers' children and had gone to church with our maid, who was Catholic. This was not unusual among German Jews, since most had assimilated to the point where they considered themselves Germans only. It was Hitler, who made us into members of a "race," relying on the painstakingly kept records of synagogues, Israelite communities, and courthouses with centuries-old documents (see certified copy in Document section).

The following is not only the story of two teenagers in isolation, facing cruelty and death; it is also a truthful account of the history of that era. I decided just lately, that none of it can hurt me any more.

3.   Who Am I?

A month after Father's death, changes happened so rapidly that I stopped asking questions. Nobody seemed to have an answer, and I assumed that we just had to live with the fact that our father was no longer with us.

Years later I learned that Mother had been forced to fight for her existence. What an uneven fight it was! Her lawyer, Otto Raab, who had good connections to the Nazi Party, tried to present her situation as a new war widow with two young children as a scandal. The license to manage her sixteen movie theaters had not been renewed. The lawyer defended her, and he wrote about the obligation of the nation towards disabled veterans, etc. None of that had any effect.

In 1937, my brother Gert applied for "*Arbeitsdienst,*" a kind of service year for young men who had graduated from high school. He was accepted without a problem. Just before he left, Mother decided to take me to a convent school in Gunzburg, where I was to receive "Holy Communion." All I remember was that Gunzburg on the Danube was such a long way from Munich that I fell asleep in the car.

When I awoke in the morning, I found myself in a large hall full of white cots. Mother was not around, neither was anybody else; everyone had gone to the usual early mass at five in the morning. I had time to cry bitterly for a long time. I could not understand why Mother had sent me away at such a time! Years later I realized that she could no longer provide a "normal life" for me. She was hoping that an orderly schedule, the companionship of children and good food would be beneficial, a better life than she could offer.

The effect on me was disastrous. The loss of my father, whom I had loved with all my childish heart, was a daily painful realization. The secrecy of our "situation" that I did not dare to mention to strangers, the absence of Mother and Gert, the strange environment, all that became such a burden that I broke down under it. Even my cat Purry would have been some comfort; what happened to my sweet little cat? No pupil was allowed to call or write home, for purposes of acclimatization. This restriction turned my hurt into an outrage!

One day, I heard two nuns talk about me as "the Jewish child." I was sitting between them on a bench, and they were discussing the latest measures against Jews. "What a crime against humanity," they were saying. "Thank God the girl does not look particularly Jewish," said Sister Lukosa. The other nun said, "I don't agree with you, her nose and her mouth are typically Jewish." I was appalled! One doesn't talk about human beings in such terms; I had never heard anything like it! There I was, sitting between them, and they discussed me as if I could not hear. Some time later, I would learn to appreciate the fact that they were on my side with their ideology, but I was too new at this, and not yet grateful for small favors.

I cried day after day and halfway through the nights. As usual, it had been my brother Gert who had anticipated a possible fiasco. When I got into the car in Munich, he embraced me and whispered: "Just in case you don't like it there, ask about my parakeet. Listen, the word 'parakeet' means that you can't stand it any longer and it means that I will come and take you home, immediately!"

Three weeks went by, and the dense cloud of depression would not lift. Any contact with the family was not allowed for two months, and the six weeks ahead of me seemed insurmountable. On a bright summer morning in June, my class was scheduled to have a field trip down to the village. While the other girls were enjoying a picnic in the park, I slipped unobserved into a phone booth nearby and dialed our number with shaking hands. I must have screamed, "Parakeet, parakeet, parakeet" into the receiver, because two days later, Mother appeared on the scene, ordered me to pack my things, and took this shadow of my former self back home.

Here too, life was not the same as I had remembered it. The absence of our father was painfully clear, Mother seemed distracted and irritable, brother Gert was constantly accompanying her to the *"Reichsfilmkammer,"* the union of the film industry, to the lawyer, to the bank, or to former colleagues in the business. Most of them kept their distance; nobody could help.

In the summer of 1935, only months after our father had died, the German Reichstag, the government, published the "Nürnberg Laws." Under threat of severe punishment and possible death sentences, it was now forbidden to ignore the difference between the true Germans or *"Reichsbürger"* and others or *"Staatsangehörige."* These two distinct groups could no longer intermarry; even extra-marital affairs were strictly punishable to the full extent of the law, possibly death.

Of course I could not grasp the significance of this second-class citizenship for Jews. I only knew that Mother had written to every German town called "Freiburg," except to the one where her family had come from. There are five or six towns in Germany by that name; from the courthouses came the desired certificate that no one by the name of Gundersheimer, mother's maiden name, was ever listed with the Israelite community or synagogue. Mother was trying to disprove her Jewish origins, a very naïve attempt to escape persecution. She told me that this would take care of the entire problem and I believed it until Nazi education at my school instructed me otherwise.

About the middle of November of the same year, vandals began to destroy Jewish stores; signs were posted, "Jews not allowed here." Mother said she was glad she didn't have our business any longer. She said she would like to move to the city center and rent a very large apartment. The rooms we would not need for ourselves, she would rent out to tourists, like a small boarding house.

"It won't be easy," she said, "but life will go on just the same." She was basically convinced that the Nazis were simply making a terrible mistake by accusing innocent people. One of these days, they would realize their wrongdoing and change their ways. After all, she had been a Red Cross nurse during the First World War, and she was the widow of a fatally wounded officer. She refused all warnings with disbelief.

"That couldn't possibly come true!" she exclaimed when anyone pointed out the clear "handwriting on the wall." I was glad to believe her when she explained to me: "I am not a racist and I am not going to become one. People's religious belief is their own and nobody's else's business. Hitler cannot prescribe how we are going to live. He can have our money. I can think of something else to make a living."

Gert's reaction was somewhat different. He was offended by the way people talked about Jews. "I will show them how wrong they are, as soon as I am old enough!" he swore. "I will take my father's place in the German army and they will get to know me better by my accomplishments. Most of all, I will tell them to leave my family in peace or they will get to feel my wrath!"

11

Gert was fifteen years old when he talked like that, and I noticed the sharp bitterness of his words. We had grown up with our father's war stories, his frightful scars, and the visible decline of his health. I never forgot what Father said about Hitler starting another war that was to be the "end of Germany." I was very much afraid for my brother when he talked about this plan to defeat the Nazis in his own way. I tried to tell him of my fear: "You'll get into the army all right," I said, "but how will you get out? You'll get out like our father did, remember!" He shrugged his shoulders and closed the conversation: "You are too young, little girl, you don't understand me."

I had my doubts that such a plan could be realized, but I didn't tell him. I felt very much alone with my pessimism and anxiety. Mother would simply not believe me, and Gert was determined to take on the Hitler regime.

For the next nine long years, Gert stuck by his daredevil plan. Writing down my memories is as much about recalling his reckless courage as it is about the history of that time.

4.   Signs of the Time

"Mother, I have quit school," I shouted and threw my books on the table. "Everybody there is making strange remarks, everybody . . . well, they are asking why I still show up every day." My mother looked so fragile all of a sudden and her face looked thinner somehow; she did not say anything, not one word. "Really," I pleaded, "I cannot go there any more. The teachers, the kids, the director, they are all trying to tell me something. It's 'you shouldn't be coming here' and 'you mustn't do that any more' and I can't take part in the play rehearsals, and I really can't do gymnastics any longer; the teacher said that she won't have me in the class."

Finally, Mother said, "You should not be exercising anyway, I will ask Dr. Zanders to write you a dispensation for your gym teacher. The P.E. is not good for you."

"But that isn't what they mean, Mother. They are getting terribly strict about it. I'm telling you, I'm through, I am not going back there!"

"Yes, you will, and by tomorrow. You mustn't try to get around schoolwork, it's so important for your future, dear."

"My future? I guess you don't believe me, do you? Look, I am supposed to get some information for this questionnaire for tomorrow and what they mostly want to know is was our father a Jew?" I was glad I had asked her at last.

"Your father was a very sick man," Mother said quietly, "and before he died, he told me to see to it that you will grow up to be a very special kind of person. For that you will need a lot of education. So, why don't you do your home-

13

work especially well tonight? You'll see that they will praise you for that, they always do."

"No, they won't," I muttered, but I didn't tell her that Lisa Isaak was expelled from my school that day, on account of her racial background. I went to my little room and just sat there for a while. I felt a clear, sharp pain in my lower abdomen. I was so alone with what I saw that day. Mother would not face the facts, and I would not be able to tell her. My head started aching. Everything went round and around. By evening I had a fever. Sweat ran down my face and back. Mother called Dr. Zanders and it was eleven o'clock that night when he took me to the hospital in his own car. "I am going to die now, " I said. I was sure of it. There wasn't anyone who understood that I was going to die. "Doctor, I am going to die now?"

"Nonsense," said Dr. Zanders. "I will take care of you and I'll have it all fixed up for you in no time, you'll see." At the hospital, a friend of Dr. Zanders took out my appendix at midnight and when I came to I was at the Zanders' big old farmhouse at Alpensee. I stayed there for several weeks and got to feeling better. I learned not to think of the past. In the meantime, my mother had enrolled me in a private school, where I was to have a good long visit with the director before starting into any classes. It would be quite all right to go there.

The director was a kind man. He told me to come for the examinations only and to study at home in between. I had a distinct feeling that he knew everything but didn't talk about it; he only said that my mother needed me at home and that he would arrange a special schedule for me. He told me to report to him once a week and that he himself would take up everything else with his teachers. Soon after that, I was known at the school as "the guest." "We have a guest today," the teacher told the class, and the students seemed to respect the arrangement. Only at school for private sessions, occasional auditing in classes and taking solitary examinations, I was able to obtain a graduation certificate during the war. I never talked to any other student. I never got into anyone's way. (See copies of two report cards in the Document section.)

At home, I tried to take care of my mother and help with our household. Mother looked like a wisp now, she had lost much weight and she stayed in bed most of the time. I must have been somewhat of a pest at times, but having just turned thirteen years of age, I didn't know it, and was convinced that I offered great comfort to her. Gert was always the one who got us to laugh, and between odd jobs, when he made a little money here and there, he became a rather good comedian.

"My goal in life" he used to say, "is not to be a father to you, because I would not want a dummy like you for a daughter. My goal in life is to become a perfect clown; I play the fool rather well, and therefore, you are to laugh immediately. So, there, that is much better, don't you think?"

5.   Invitation to the Lion's Den

Not until my name was called did I fully realize that this was the Gestapo headquarters of our city; while I sat there waiting for several hours one warm summer afternoon, I repeated over and over in my mind what my old Uncle Otto had said when he was told about my notice to appear here. "In case anything goes wrong, give me a call and I'll be right over from my office." His office was in the huge square complex of the state's Department of Justice, and dear old Otto was not really my uncle. He was a city attorney and the self-proclaimed protector of my family of three; he had helped to pull us through so many times already, that it seemed to me whenever Uncle Otto's gray goatee started quivering, things always took a turn for the better.

It was the summer of 1937; I was fourteen years old and a very childish girl at that. "Really, all I need to do is to call Uncle Otto," I reassured myself, while I handed my "Notice to Appear" to a clerk behind a milk glass window. She looked at it, gave it back to me, and motioned me over to the next door; she closed the door behind me and told me to sit down on a bench by the wall; then she returned to her typewriter. I looked at this card, which had INVITATION printed on it in large black letters. "Mother said that this would be just a routine sort of thing," I reminded myself. "I should stop turning some dumb little INVITATION to appear into a big deal. I had best think of something funny."

The steady clicking of the clerk's typewriter made me a bit sleepy, maybe it was the heat in the large whitewashed office. How much this room resembled any other office! What was the joke again that our friends were telling about the Palace of Justice? That's where Uncle Otto had his office. Yes, now I remembered, "Why do the Germans need such a huge palace for their law offices when all they have left now is such a lousy little bit of justice?"

From time to time, someone came into the room from adjoining offices to talk to the clerk or to answer the telephone. A secretary was loudly discussing a house search and arrest notice with two men. I heard one of them saying. "Get out the folder on these people, inform the driver, and set the time of arrest at 2:00 A.M." I blew my nose with a loud noise because something hot had just welled up into my head.

One of the men came toward me. "Who is she?" I went through both my pockets, came up with the card and with another handkerchief kept blowing my nose. "Come over here," he said. I handed him the postcard that had INVITATION printed on it. Then I heard myself saying "Thank you for the invitation." Walking along behind him, the whole scene became engraved in my mind in a most unusual way, as if I would never be able to forget this again; there was a message to myself, always to be remembered: *If I get out of here before night, I must never tell Mother or Gert what I heard here, or what happened. This is real trouble and I will spare them the fear of it.*

"You are the daughter of the Jewish widow Sarah Gundersheimer?" The voice came from behind a large desk. "You were born in Stalldorf near here? You are fourteen years old?" "Yes." "Do you have anything to say for yourself?" "No." Long silence . . . I had not yet looked up at this voice that came from inside a black uniform. "Why do you think we have asked you to appear?" "I got this postcard, I think. . . . I mean, I think it said INVITATION on it . . . so I came over. " I could see his shiny boot behind one side of the desk. "Thank you for the invitation," I said. His voice sounded less official now, when he said, "It's is up to me to see to it that you get the right idea."

Then he started reading off a list of rules for conduct, all those things that I could not do, places where I was never to be seen, people whom I could never get near to, what to expect if found trespassing on sacred German rights, etc. "You are to avoid carefully any contact with members of the Aryan race. Never, and I mean never, are you to converse with young people from the Hitler Youth. Never are you to be found speaking to a member of the German armed forces or the National Socialist party, to a member of this, or a member of that . . ." There followed a long list of organizations. I kept nodding my head, trying not to remember any of them.

"We have to make sure," he went on, "that we keep our sacred nation pure, come what may, we cannot take any chances with the enemies of our sacred German fatherland. We have no choice but to follow through, as far as our sacred German heritage is concerned."

Silence. "I admit that this whole thing is probably not your fault, even though I suppose that we can't be sure about anything." He went on in sort of a jovial mood, almost friendly. "I think it was probably your father's fault, you should have left Germany long before it came to this. All I know for sure is that it certainly isn't my fault. Quite the contrary: I consider this to be a favor I am doing you, to be giving you plenty of warning, way ahead of time. You are still too young to understand any of it, and I rather think it was mostly your father's fault, leaving you unprotected in a hostile world. Let me tell you that I, too, would not be sitting here in front of you, if only my father had left me something to get a start with in this world.

"As it stands, I never had anything to live on, never, do you hear me, and I have to do a lot of things that I don't especially cherish doing. I consider myself lucky to have ended up in the devoted service of our beloved Führer. Whatever you are going to be some day, a Jewish bitch or some such thing . . . do you think that I enjoy in the least what I am doing? Look at me!"

I did see a heavy, round figure in black uniform, a bald, bloated, grayish face over it. He seemed very old to my fourteen years of experience, with puffed-up cheeks overhanging a tight collar. "I am sorry." I heard myself saying it again.

Silence. "I have already told you that I am not a happy man. I have the extraordinary pleasure of giving you fair warning way ahead of time. If you give us any more problems than we have on our hands already, you are going to be put away for good. Don't think that some nice-looking kid from the Storm Staffel is going to be of any help to you, that all you have to do is start a little something with a smart young guy from the armed forces and you've got it made; don't think you are a step ahead of us, because it won't work, do you hear? You might as well find that out right here. We are going to nip that problem in the bud right now. Do you understand?"

"No. . . . I mean, I don't know what you mean. . . . I don't understand; maybe I'm too young to know all that much, but I'll try to remember what you said, really, I will. . . . I'll try not to get into anybody's way, I promise. . . ."

This was followed by another list of rules for conduct, but all I could hear at this point was that I had to sign some identification card or papers. "You are to carry this card at all times," he went on and on. "Pick up the card next door, and keep it on you at all times. That way we'll know at least who you are." I got up and started toward the door. "Are you through now, huh?" He sounded quite unpleasant again. "Yes, " I turned around and faced him once more, "I do not wish to bother you and I really am sorry. I mean I am very sorry about . . . well, about what you told me today . . . I mean I am very sorry about your father."

I was able to sign something, and then I was outside and trying to open my bicycle lock. The blasted bicycle lock would not open. I turned it and twisted it, and the key kept falling on the pavement. Maybe I would not be able to ride home just now? Maybe I could just sit down for a while, on the ground. I must call my mother right now, I remembered. She had a way of looking ashen, old and tired whenever there was something going with the Gestapo; she would worry until she heard from me. I better call her and tell her that I got through it all right. Especially since everything went rather well!

The bicycle lock opened, and I pushed the bike along the sidewalk to the nearest telephone booth. The farther I walked away from the Gestapo building, the better I felt. "Really, Mutti, nothing happened, nothing at all! I didn't even have to call Uncle Otto! Is Gert home? I need to see him right away, about something, I'll tell you later. Give Topsy a kiss from me, and tell her I'm all right and I'm going to take her for a walk when I get home."

I was off the phone. Topsy was our dachshund, and she was my doll-baby! I didn't play with dolls any more. Her favored place was my father's big chair, where she spent quite a bit of time. Not a day went by that I didn't think about my father. He was a persistent memory now.

6.　　Grandmother Clothilde

Again and again people came to say good-bye before their departure from Germany. It became increasingly more impossible to stay, and the sooner one left, the more one could take along. Since 1934, I had one uncle and aunt in Paraguay, another in Chile; the youngest of my uncles, Eugen, left so late, he had to fish for pearls somewhere on the South American coast in order to get a start. The black sheep of the family, Ernst, went to France one step ahead of the German army, where he stayed hidden in the south. He returned in the summer of 1945, weeks after the war ended.

I had always sensed somehow that my mother had a definite aversion towards all of them. She had mentioned casually that her father had been a terrible tyrant and that his money was a hateful and threatening part of her younger days. This is perhaps why I did not meet any of my relatives until Hitler's Gestapo drove them into hiding. The first time I met my grandmother was when she came to live with us for several months. At that time she was waiting for her visa to Paraguay, to live there with her oldest son.

The only thing my mother said about "Oma" at that time was that she had hated my dad, convinced that he was after their money. From this bit of information, I concluded that she must have had some. When she moved in with us, however, my feelings of rejection of her gave way to her constant tears. She was fearful of being arrested; she seemed old and homeless to me. When it was time for her to leave the country, I felt very close to her. Was there anything I could give her before this awesome trip to another continent, something that would remind her of me? She wore the most beautiful jewelry I had ever seen, and it did seem odd to me that she would still wear her precious pearls every day, at a time when her son was forced to dive into the ocean for such treasures.

When it was time to say good-bye to her, I had the feeling that I would never see her again; I ran upstairs to my room sobbing and sat there quietly fighting the tears. My mother was calling for me to come back down to see Oma leave. There was not a thing I could do about it, nothing I could add. I looked about my room. On the bookshelf stood a tiny hand-carved manger scene that a friend had given me some time ago. It was exquisite work! On the smallest of space stood the babe's simple crib with the mother behind it, tiny sheep lying all around, the wooden roof gracefully sheltered the scene.

I took it downstairs with me. "Here is shelter for you, my dearest Oma, and may you find happiness and peace, in the foreign country far away." She wrapped it in a handkerchief and put it in her handbag. Then she left, crying. She never returned to Germany. I never saw her again. She wrote to us from Paraguay via the Swiss Red Cross.

In one of these letters, she said that my manger scene became her most prized possession because she had become a Christian. Not until I got this letter did it occur to me that I had given my Jewish grandmother the carved sculpture that represented the birth of Jesus.

Those were awful times, when Hitler's agents were running about trying to catch a lot of people. Almost every one of our relatives was leaving the country to escape this insane situation. The good-byes were almost always forever. Grandparents, uncles, aunts and cousins we now no longer had. We definitely felt the danger in staying. For some reason we learned to live with it.

7. The Last Year before World War II

Our home in the Pettenkoferstrasse was a number of rectangular rooms strung together by a dark, narrow corridor on the seventh floor of an old downtown apartment house. Opposite those rooms with high windows that looked down on the street side were the kitchen, the bathroom, and a large closet. My mother, always in need of additional income, rented out every available corner except the living room, where she slept on a couch. My brother Gert shared a room with one of the renters or boarders, who changed frequently; they had to be carefully selected as to background, political views, and personal convictions. Our whole "situation," as we preferred to call it, was getting shakier by the day; not long before, a measure had been passed that we could no longer rent our own apartment, let alone sublease rooms to anyone else. Were we going to be homeless?

I still inhabited the closet by the kitchen. I made a two-level home out of it by removing the lower part of a bunk and setting my most precious possession under my bed: an ancient sewing machine. The arrangement, engineered by my brother, eliminated the space problem, but it left the bed with only one of the lower slats; however, I was used to moving around very carefully and being cautious about anything and anybody. The boy next door, for instance, who had first spent much time hanging out of his back window talking to me, turned out to belong to the Hitler Youth. The things he talked about got on my nerves considerably. Later on, when we had to move away, I imagined that his father had spoken to the manager about us and that it would have been better for the three of us had I not started talking to him. The manager told us that someone in the immediate neighborhood had complained about our living there and I was afraid that the nice kid next door had been the cause for this; by that time it was too late to even think about it and we moved away fast. I would have to be more careful in the future.

Meanwhile, the city was enjoying a successful tourist summer. The crisis in Czechoslovakia had passed without incident; Mr. Chamberlain, Monsieur Daladier, and Mussolini had been working together to avoid the outbreak of a war, and school had let out early on the day of another political victory for Hitler. The streets were hung with banners, the parades were colorful, the bands were playing, and tourists were pouring into town to take part in numerous festivities. My mother was able to keep every room rented on short terms, which was best as far as our privacy was concerned. We took in out-of-town travelers who were stranded without room reservations and were glad to find a bed unexpectedly. The summer was easier for us, always, with special opera performances, theater summer season, and many foreign guests in town, who would stay a week or two and then leave without asking a lot of questions.

In the springtime, my mother had been ill for six weeks. Dr. Zanders said that she had a tumor, which caused internal bleeding; when she finally got up from her living-room couch again after six long weeks, she was weaker than I had ever seen her.

More than before, I helped with all the housework and renting of the rooms, even though I have since had my doubts as to the efficiency of my assistance. This too was easier in the summer with no schoolwork on my mind, but I was a silly young girl and probably not much help to her. My brother kept us laughing; he burlesqued critical situations, clowned all the time, and took nothing seriously, least of all ourselves. Our mother got to feeling better as the summer went on, which was by far the most important thing of all, since she could not be admitted to any hospital on account of our "situation." Hospitals, like public transportation, were too dangerous for us to take a chance, being checked frequently by Hitler's police.

During one of these summers before the outbreak of the Second World War, I met my first American. I awakened early one morning, slipped into the kitchen, and sleepily started to turn the crank of our coffee grinder. The aroma of freshly ground beans smelled delightful in the dawn's gray light. Suddenly, I heard a loud, deep groan from behind the kitchen table. I stopped turning the crank and tiptoed to the window, where I took a glance behind the bare wood of the tabletop, and saw two dirty feet on our kitchen bench.

Probably one of Gert's friends, I figured and continued working the coffee grinder. The person on our bench turned around; and a stubbly beard became visible at the other end of the blanket. Down the corridor I ran, into the living room and to Mother's bed. "There is a filthy-looking man sleeping on the kitchen bench!" "It's just a young student from an American university," my mother explained. "He was stone drunk last night, he could not even remember where he had left his bike, let alone find himself a place to sleep. Go and wake up your brother and tell him to take care of his friend."

Gert and the fearsome-looking stranger left to locate the lost bicycle. When they returned later in the morning, the stranger, still covered with mud, disappeared in the direction of the bathroom where he spent what seemed like the rest of the day. All he had with him was a small backpack, but when he emerged after hours of showering, shaving and grooming, he was like a different person. In his white shirt and pressed summer denims, he bowed toward us gracefully and introduced himself as John Allison, Junior. To me, it was an unforgettable lesson on the meaning of outward appearances. I had never seen anyone change so completely in a relatively short time.

After supper that night, the young man took my knitting out of my hands and added several rows very neatly; by watching me he had just learned how to knit. I thought this was unusual! Nobody I knew would have done a thing like that, to be sure. The next day, he washed his dirty clothes and that too I had never seen a man do for himself. He stayed another night on the kitchen bench since we did not have a bed available, and then he left to continue his bicycle tour of Europe.

8.   Beginning of the War

In the summer of 1939, the Goethe Institute for Foreign Studies had arranged for us to pick up two students from the University of Michigan at the railway station. The girls were to arrive on the evening train from Zurich and could be recognized by their white summer dresses and by red carnations in their hands. We were just debating the possibility of many summer travelers in white dresses, who might by chance be carrying flowers, when our telephone rang.

On the other end of the line was someone from the American consulate, informing us that the two young ladies were to be accompanied to the next train back to Switzerland that very evening! The reason for this inhospitable attitude was stated very briefly: immediate danger of war. An official declaration of war was expected from the German government within a few days, and the U.S. Consulate was advising all American travelers to leave Germany for the time being.

We found this message so distressing that we didn't think of asking for a written statement from the consulate, and when we met our two world travelers at the station, we found them unwilling to believe in the catastrophe. They insisted that they had paid in advance for their two weeks' stay, that they were not about to be scared out of a long-planned summer vacation. They had no hotel reservations in Zurich. They decided they would go to Austria if they really had to leave because at least they had not seen Austria as yet!

We spent all evening with them at the station restaurant, refusing to take them home with us and trying to explain to them their good fortune in having been forewarned. We could not get anyone at the consulate on the phone, because the number was busy all evening. Whether we were finally getting through to them or whether the evening newscast contained a confirmation of the rumor, they did at last take the problem seriously enough to arrange for their return to Zurich that night. From the departing train, they assured us that they did not believe any of it and that they would be back soon. When they had finally left it became increasingly clear to us how much we would have liked to be in their place.

The next day, August 31, 1939, brought restrictions concerning almost everything: Use of the Autobahn, of trains, planes, gasoline. Military units were being moved across the country, all summer activities came to a sudden stop. The first day of September made it all official: War had been declared. The *blitzkrieg* into Poland was beginning.

I felt as if the ground under my feet had been removed. What was ahead for us now? Nobody knew, of course, but one could guess. Some of our friends seemed to have an idea of all that was waiting for us in the near future. The announcements made over the radio were bold and proud as those of a nation at the beginning of war. Victory talk and march music seemed to drown out small voices of reason. Within me, I could hear the painful question: How much death, how much destruction, how much despair, and how much misery would this war cause in our lifetime?

We did not hear from our two girls again and never found out whether their travel agent was able to arrange a different tour for them. Perhaps they spent their entire vacation in Switzerland. Switzerland, how far away it seemed, and yet it was so close to us geographically.

9.   No More School

My sixteenth birthday was extremely depressing; I was not sure just why; perhaps it was the approaching end of my schooling. "*Mittelschule*" ended with the ninth grade, and what I would do after that was anybody's guess. Actually everybody was depressed after the outbreak of the Second World War, which my father once called the beginning of the end. Long before the actual end of the school year in July, Mother applied for me at many different institutions. The next three years of schooling led to the "Abitur," a necessary step for entering higher education at an academy, college or university. Mother was optimistic, as usual. "You'll see, everything will turn out good for you."

In fact, everything turned out completely negative for me. We tried four different institutions, Anna Schule, Luisen Gymnasium, the Art Academy, School of Fashion (*Meisterschule für Mode*); all demanded a paper that I did not have, the "*arische Nachweis*" (Proof of Aryan heritage).

We tried the Munich theaters. Mother thought I could learn to design and sew costumes. The reply was that all state theaters were supervised by the Minister of Propaganda, Dr. Goebbels, and were unable to employ me for that reason. I endured one refusal after another. Finally there was an acceptance at the Fashion-Salon of the Countess Warnberg. Her establishment had a very good reputation, and she was charming and understanding. I was to start as an apprentice right after the end of the school year.

I was not enthusiastic about an apprenticeship that

would last three years. However, I was aware of the fact that nothing else had materialized; at least I would be among friendly people. As soon as I had gotten used to the idea, on the third or fourth day at the workplace, the Gestapo suddenly appeared and arrested the cutter. She was a fragile little woman who insisted that she was completely innocent; but she was Jewish and the scene was gruesome. I was immediately traumatized and felt sick. My stomach began to turn on me and I rushed to the restroom to throw up.

There was a very narrow window that looked down into the back alley. I managed to wriggle out through the tiny opening and dropped down hard on the cement. At least I didn't have to go back to the horrible scene inside. I ran all the way home to the Pettenkoferstrasse and declared that I would not work there. I could not go back because the Gestapo would surely come there again. "I am not going to sit there until they come and arrest me." With these words I gave my poor mother a terrible problem to solve. She had no idea what to suggest for me! I was sixteen years old, had to stop school three years early and had no place to go.

Gert did his very best to cheer us up. One night he entered the living room wearing the greatcoat of the German army. I remember that he had bought the thing second hand. He put on his stone face, clicked his heels, and bellowed: "You are the widow Sara?" Then he opened his coat and proudly displayed my mother's corset, the bra stuffed, the garters dangling. We started laughing uncontrollably. He turned his eyes toward heaven piously and squeaked with a soft, piercing voice; "Yes, I am the one." As the dialogue between the officer and his victim unfolded, we fell off our chairs laughing. "Don't you think I am an excellent actor?" asked Gert. "I love to play this idiot, because I do it so well! Also, I try to make you laugh because it's about time you did!" He took off the greatcoat of the German army and turned slowly like a peacock to show off my mother's corset.

Gert had enlisted for service in the German army, but was told that he would have to wait his turn. They would expect him to bring the necessary papers, among them the proof of Aryan heritage (*arische Nachweis*). In order to fill the time, he applied at the University of Munich for his first semester of chemistry. While filling out an application, he heard that they needed help with registration. Soon he sat behind one of the windows with all the stamps at his disposal. The first thing he accomplished on the job was to give himself the necessary forms and then he stamped them, proof of Aryan heritage included!

After one semester of studying chemistry, Gert was drafted into the army and he used the same papers, the ones he had stamped himself, to evade inquiries concerning his status as a member of the Aryan race. "This is a bunch of twirled shit anyway," he explained. "As long as they can go crazy like that, so can I!" His main objective accomplished, namely to wear the uniform, he only had to volunteer for the upcoming war effort, and the protection of his family would be effective. He was going to beat them with their own methods: The mother and sister of a German soldier fighting at the front for the Fatherland would be safe from deportation. This was not quite the way it turned out, but it was the first step in a number of tricks and deceptions he used.

Gert had just about convinced us to breathe a little easier, when a new proclamation forced us into immediate action. Security measures were being tightened, and one by one, our rights were taken away. In the same mailbox that held my mother's small pension as a war widow, we found frequent notifications of new restrictions. Jews were no longer allowed to use public transportation, parks, and movie-houses, even the Munich Zoo! "What could be in the zoo that we can't go there?" I wondered.

The newest was now that Jews could no longer rent housing, and at the same time, it was forbidden for landlords to rent to Jewish people. This was a blow that we could not ignore, because we needed the income from our house guests. My mother's small pension was not enough to live on. A notice from our landlord arrived, with the eviction effective immediately. We did not have the slightest idea what we would do or where we would go. For the first time, Mother's optimism was no longer plausible; we had to face that we were desperate because we had to give up our only home.

In fact, two years later the first bombs that fell in Munich included a direct hit into the apartment house where we had lived on the fifth floor. All that remained of Pettenkoferstrasse #5 was an enormous hole in the ground. I never forgot the moral of the story: When excluded or thrown out, remember that it can turn out to be a blessing. Yet we could not see the wisdom of the latest development at the time; it looked as if we would soon be homeless.

Jewish families were forced into specially prepared housing. Mother's reaction was again a stern disbelief. No way in heaven or on earth would she oblige with such a move. Not once did she consider defeat! Her attitude was decisive for all that was to follow, because these Jewish settlements were the basis for the removal of Jewish people to undisclosed locations in Eastern Europe. We did not know the fate awaiting us, but we could sense it. Gert and Mother spent long evenings in devising a plan to escape, after I was sent to bed. I was told complete lies and half-truths, was given sleeping pills to knock me out, but the storm that was to blow us away could be observed on the horizon.

The "Final Solution to the Jewish Problem" was officially authorized at Wannsee, Berlin, on January 20, 1942. A decree originated from the *Reichsministerium* that stated; "All assets of deported Jews are confiscated by the Gestapo. Jews can keep 100 Marks and 50kg of baggage each." How could such a decree be implemented? The creation of Jewish settlements in Munich had begun two years earlier, in a suburb called Milbertshofen.

In the fall of 1941, eighteen barracks housed about one thousand people. The first transport to a concentration camp left on November 20, 1941. Almost one thousand people were on this train, the same people who had been forced weeks earlier to move into the barracks at Knorrstrasse 148 in Milbertshofen.

When the landlord evicted us from the apartment, we didn't know about the deportations that were to follow, but the systematic harassment grew unmistakably in a certain direction. One could assume that these settlements or ghettos would not be the end of the process. From there, people could be forcibly removed without causing a commotion among the rest of the population. The barracks would then be ready to isolate another set of unfortunate occupants.

Of Munich's six thousand Jewish citizens, eighty-three were still alive after the Second World War; all the others had been told that they would have to work for the war effort. Since they were forbidden to work quite a bit earlier, most were hopeful that their life would improve in these work camps. Nothing was known about the gas chambers.

The three of us decided not to make it easy for them. The earliest of the transport orders stated that Mother would be taken to an old people's home in Theresienstadt (Terrezin) and that there was a music camp for children there. To suspect a bald-faced lie was not difficult because Mother was forty-seven years old at the time. She said "Do they expect me to believe this? I am not too old to remember that I was born in 1895 and it shows me what they are. I am going to stay right here and fight this." My brother kept saying: "The only way to fight the Gestapo is to cheat and confuse them."

10.　　Homeless

A friend of my mother's, who had spent several years with us when we were both young girls, came to our rescue. Helen and her husband, Frank, for whom money did not seem any object, offered to buy a small house for us. They would register the place as their own residence; for all inquiries, we would be taking care of this house temporarily for them and we would be living there without being haunted by a landlord.

Our "angels of mercy" arrived days later for the purpose of buying us a house in the suburbs. To my amazement, they acted as if this was no problem for them. Frank was the owner of a large wine and champagne business; he was high up in the Nazi party and maintained numerous connections to the SS and Gestapo. He was one of those early Nazis, who had joined up as a young fellow and had used his membership to his business advantage. Some of these early Nazis (his membership number was #123) were not at all in agreement with later Nazi policy, were against the war, against Nazi methods and against their racism.

I found it hard to believe when he said: "Your newest predicament is not a problem for me. Number one, I don't like the way our government is dealing with some people lately; secondly, I can easily open a branch office of my business in Munich and buy a place to house it. Thirdly, real estate is one of the best investments I can think of. You'll be safe there; my party connections can pull this atrocity to a happy ending."

Our most pressing problem, a place to stay, was so easily solved by this kind man. He was about thirty-five, looked older then that because of his weight; he was round and short, heavy about the middle with a receding hairline. *This too is a Nazi,* I thought to myself. He bought a townhouse the following day, near the West Cemetery on the outskirts of Munich.

The next lesson learned: there are different types of Nazis, after all. It occurred to me; once one joined the party as a young guy, one could not say, "As of next week, I won't be a party member any more, I quit!" Persecution, even death, would follow such a move. Nobody could leave the party, the SS or the Gestapo, it would be suicide. Not only that, I heard people talking about the torture chambers that existed in the basement of Gestapo headquarters on the corner of Briennerstrasse and Tuerkenstrasse.

I heard Hitler in one of his many speeches say these words: "Those who are not for me, are against me, and we will not tolerate them!" Many friends and relatives were leaving the country, to France, to New York, to South America. Our cousin Werner Demuth was deported to Auschwitz, where he died at the age of twenty-six. We knew all too well, what was happening. The reason we did not talk about it: we were completely helpless; reminding each other of that fact made it even worse. Leaving the country would mean that we wouldn't know the language, would have no friends and certainly no money. Mother decided against it.

The house in the suburbs was a quiet lovely place. Surrounded by open fields, it was actually three houses under one roof, part of a huge project of town houses that was interrupted by the war. Brand new, modern and sunny, it was just the place to make my mother feel better. It had a small garden out in back and a balcony off the living room, so we could be outside in the fresh air and visit with our neighbors.

Around seven one morning, we saw a long black limousine stop in front of our new place. Two young SS officers jumped out and stood at attention by the parked car: This was, without a doubt, government transportation! The front door next to ours fell shut, and the sound of military boots came down the few steps below my window; then we saw a man in black uniform get into the back seat, the two officers took the front seats, and the limousine rolled away, right by our unbelieving eyes.

"May I introduce to you, beloved sister," my brother said in his very best sarcasm, "to a rather high officer of the Storm Staffel also known as our next door neighbor?" Some surprise this was! Soon, his lovely young wife made an introductory visit at our house, together with their four little sons whom she called *"Ferkelchen"* or piglets. She laughed a great deal and in a peculiar way, starting in a very high tone of voice and then sounding down the scale, each laugh ending with the same melodious gurgle. Ha-ha-ha-he-he-he-he-ho-hu-hu-hu-hu-gli-gli-gli!

We sat up half the following night, trying to figure out what we should do now. Mother was worried. "If this man doesn't like it," she said, "it could become a terrible problem for us." My brother was much more optimistic: "They are going to like it," he said cheerfully. "These houses are so expensive now, since all construction was halted on account of the war; so nobody, and I mean nobody at all is going to suspect that we are the so-called enemies of the people, unless we tell them ourselves!"

He seemed to find this prospect amusing. "We are going to tell these fancy neighbors of ours that we've just paid cash for this joint, and that I am waiting for my draft call from the army." "But, Gert, what happens when that call never comes and they must begin to wonder why you are the only young man in all of Munich who is still at home?" I did not even want to stay another day. "Mother is so right," I insisted, we would never get away with that. "Keep your big mouth shut," my brother said lovingly, "and everything will be all right, because I can handle this situation. I got it all figured out!" he announced. "Oh, you have, have you?" I was getting more curious. "Would you mind telling us?"

"Well—" Gert grinned—"you see, everybody thinks it is going to be a long war. That means it is going to be fairly easy to get into the army, the difficult part is how to get out again, once I'm in." For the moment we felt safer than we had in some time, and since we never could think very far ahead into the future, we let it go at that.

We were to live next to the Fruhlich family during the five remaining years of the war. Our dealings with them we kept to the absolute minimum, since we never felt at ease with them. Father Fruhlich really was pretty high up there in ranks with the Nazi government, an SS *Obergruppenführer*, to be exact. He was also one of the few whom no one could figure out. To the day when the American CIC arrested him, he remained strange, impenetrable and aloof, wearing his uniform at a time when the Nazis were trying to be civilians or to get away. When the American jeeps drove up, he was out there in SS uniform; digging up his flowerbeds, waiting for them; but that was five long years after we moved in next to him, and what happened in the meantime was incredible. At one time, he may have saved our lives, but even that was not at all sure.

A third of the townhouse was inhabited by a lawyer's widow and her three children. The mother was a stout and resolute lady from East Prussia; when the city was bombed for the first time, she took over the function of "air-raid-warden," or "*Luftschutzwart*." We called her "Aunt

Luschuwa," which was short for Luftschutzwart, but sounded somewhat Polish as she did herself and therefore, fit her very well; she kept this name "Luschwa" to the present day and also always retained the friendship she found with my mother. It wasn't longer than a week after moving in that we told her about our desperate situation, our fear of being taken to one of the many camps some night, and our misgivings about living next to the big SS wheel.

"I and my children will be of great help to you," she said in response to our story, "With God's help I will watch over you; I will inform you of anything that is going on in the neighborhood. I will feed you and entertain you, and you will be safe here. I will not let them take you! Put on the coffee pot!" We made a pact that was never to be broken. Many of the happier moments during the years of the war were spent with the great "Luschuwa" and her three rascally kids.

11.   Mobilization

"Now we are going to finally have it!" said Gert cheerfully. "The war has started, and it is my time to get into the army." All young men were getting drafted. Excitement was in the air, especially among family and friends of the soldiers-to-be. An entire nation mobilizing was not something I could fight with my fear. I decided to see Gert's point of view, and some of his courage rubbed off on me.

His plan was about to be realized. The papers he had given himself while helping with registration at the university, he submitted for induction as a volunteer. This student of chemistry with good grades would be valuable for the war effort. The required "Proof of Aryan Heritage" was stamped by the University of Munich, actually by Gert himself. He was accepted to serve in a special unit to be trained for communications, located at Stuttgart.

We took him to the train station, and I couldn't stop my tears during the farewell embrace. "I guarantee you the Gestapo will leave us in peace now, they wouldn't dare raise a conflict with the army in time of war, I know exactly what I am doing and I am not afraid. You shouldn't be afraid either. All is well and the way I wanted it."

The train pulled out of the station like so many other trains. I managed a smile and waved. It was then that Mother started crying. When the train was gone, I found a lot of words to comfort her, but I did not believe in them myself. Soon, letters kept coming and going.

12.   Something Does Not Add Up

Gert's great sense of humor and unshakable optimism would be sharply missed. We did not even hear from him now. I think he was stationed in Flensburg, on the most northern German peninsula, bordering on Denmark. This place was far away from the Alpine region that was our home; we felt a painful void again. I assumed that the loss would bring Mother and me closer together. No such thing was occurring. What really happened was quite the opposite of my expectations.

My mother, deeply unhappy at that time, criticized me constantly. Mostly she complained that I did not find something to do. This was much easier said than done. The Nazis were everywhere, the safest place was at home, reading books and helping with the household. We were still renting out rooms to various boarders; I remember two young guys who were waiting to be drafted; after three or four weeks they left for the Eastern Front and we found out later that they both died, Walter and Klaus.

I thought I was keeping busy at home, but Mother was not satisfied. Then came a phone call from Helen and Frank Becker, our benefactors and friends. About two months earlier, they had had their first child, a baby boy named Johann. Mother and Helen decided without my knowledge that I should help take care of the new baby and live with the Becker family for a while. Mother was most enthusiastic and exclaimed that this was a godsend for me. Helen had praised me as reliable and trustworthy enough to relieve her. She would be able to leave the house more, go shopping, help with the winery, or visit relatives and friends.

Number one, I was happy to be helpful to these great friends of ours. We were living in their house without paying rent. Secondly, it would be fun to take care of the child; I loved little kids and was sure I could do quite well. Above it all loomed the fact that there was nothing else attainable without guidance or directives. Of course I agreed to do my very best; I was excited about my new life. I was told that Frank had some business in Munich the following week and that I could ride with him to Rastadt, my new home.

Mother was obviously relieved; she counted all the reasons why I should be happy about this latest development. "They have everything at the winery; you'll get good food and you really won't have to work hard. Taking care of a baby will be such fun for you; you deserve a little happiness after getting out of school. Don't worry about me, I will be fine."

Full of anticipation, I got into Frank Becker's Opel and passed the time by reading a book. I tried not to talk and distract the driver; Becker did not seem interested in what I had to say, so I pretended to read. I noticed that we were not driving toward Stuttgart and Baden, but that we got off the Autobahn where a sign read: "Bodensee." I asked the driver: "We are going to Lindau/Bodensee?" "No," he said, "I have to check on a business deal at Ravensburg and if the gentleman I need to see is not available tonight, we'll have to stay at the hotel until tomorrow."

My heartbeat became noticeably fast; I had the distinct feeling that he was lying. It sounded phony. There was a long silence, because I decided that I could not start an argument with my driver. Finally, in a calm and casual tone, I remarked that I had no money for a hotel, not one cent. "I just hope they have a room for us at the hotel, never mind the money," he replied. Immediately, my anticipation for my new life turned sour. He had not told Mother that he would stay at Ravensburg. To be sure, there was nothing I could do about it, but I tried once more: "Does Helen know about this?" He said, "I'll call her this evening." Obviously, she did not know about this.

Nobody knows, I thought, *because the businessman in Ravensburg does not exist.* I wished that I were still at home, because the present situation was not a good one; but it was too late for such contemplations. I had best read my book and hope for the businessman to show up after all. I could still be wrong to worry.

An hour later, just before Ravensburg, Frank Becker reached, resolutely, with his hand under my skirt. I suppressed the impulse to hit him with my book! Not a good idea, so I just stuck the closed book between my legs and moved as close to the car door as I could. Nobody said a word until we arrived at the hotel. It was about six o'clock, just before dark. He told me to stay in the car until he had checked with the reception desk. I knew before he came back that there would only be one room available. I was not prepared, however, for his train of thought: "The one room is fine with me, because it is less expensive that way." I was keenly aware that I could not make it more expensive for him by calling the police.

My thoughts went around and around in my head: *I bet this last available room does not have single beds. I am now the main character in a terribly bad second-rate movie! This is our benefactor, our angel of mercy, and he seems to have another side to him that was not anticipated! What do I do next? Call my mother? Call his wife? What if they are not home? I have no money for the phone! Maybe he'll let me call, maybe he is nicer than I expected. What if I made such a scene that he loses his adventurous spirit? That's it. I'll have to talk him out of it, and he is not a mean-natured fellow as far as I can tell. He does have a good side to him; it will turn out all right after all.*

We ate in the dining room silently, and it made me feel better because I had been hungry. Upstairs in the hotel room, I claimed to be very tired and occupied my place in the big bed, as close to the edge as I could. He left the light on when he climbed into the bed on the other side and presently scooted over close to me. "Good God!" I screamed. "This couldn't possibly come true!" (My mother's repeated expression.)

I pushed him away with both my feet and rolled out of the bed. I fell into the armchair next to the bed. I demanded to call my mother. He was sitting in a chair on the far side of the room, and he looked at me sadly, with the eyes of a beaten dog. He began a long speech: "Your mother cannot help you. Your mother is my responsibility, as you well know. Your mother was mighty glad when we offered to take you in. You are making trouble for her when you are mean to me. Most of all, this scene you are making is no fun for me, no fun at all!"

I started to cry. "Frank, how come you consider this fun? You are too old for me and you have a wife and a new baby," I sobbed. "Please tell me why you could possibly have fun frightening me like that. I am just a kid."

His answer was spontaneous as if he was prepared for accusations of that nature: "I am not an angel," he explained. "If I were an angel, I would be in heaven. I am not an angel, but I am not the devil either and as long as you have this hateful attitude and apparently an aversion toward me, just go back to bed and sleep. I need to call my business-friend; I'll be downstairs for a while."

When he returned a few minutes later, I pretended to be asleep. I was deeply grateful that he had responded positively and his remark about the devil reminded me of a drama I had read several times, Goethe's *Faust:* young Grete was seduced by the devil to fall in love with Faust and she killed herself when she got pregnant and her lover left her. It was definitely a good sign that Frank had said he was not the devil. I thought, *Tomorrow, he will be home with his wife and child and he won't want me to talk to Helen about all this.* Actually, he was right about my mother, I was glad that I didn't call and give her additional trouble. She had plenty as it was. I fell asleep satisfied that I had handled a crisis like an adult.

In the morning at the restaurant, Frank gave me some of his breakfast; I asked him to order a cup of hot cocoa for me, please. "You know you do not deserve it, and I am expected to pay for your unpleasant manners yet." Was this the same person who bought a house for us, so we could live in peace? I would have to talk to Mother and Helen both, as soon as we arrive in Rastadt. With his peculiar set of morals, Frank was somebody to fear.

13. At Risk

At about eleven o'clock the next morning, we arrived at the winery. It was more like an estate. The first thing I noticed after getting out of the car was a big hose laid across the driveway; where one hose was connected to another, wine was leaking out and two dogs were busy slurping up the wine as it dripped down. The mansion had a circular staircase; every room seemed very big to me. Helen showed me her darling baby, Johann, who was sleeping. At lunch, a young lieutenant by the name of Paul Hoffman sat next to her. I understood that he was awaiting his orders and was spending this free time at the Beckers' winery.

My attention was focused on the two-month-old child. I enjoyed my new job tremendously and soon became emotionally attached to the little boy. Soon, Helen could leave without worry, visit friends in the evening, help in the business office, or go shopping in the nearby city. She had a lot of clothes made and had to go to fittings quite often. It wasn't long before she moved the baby's bed into my big room and I was proud to play my important role with such success!

On an ordinary Friday afternoon, Helen stood in the entrance hall with a packed suitcase and surprised me with the explanation that she was going to spend the weekend at the newly purchased hunting lodge in the Black Forest. I was horror-stricken with fear of being in charge of her son all by myself. I demanded the time to ask some questions before her departure: the phone number of her pediatrician, for example. She replied that Klara, the maid, had all the necessary information, that Klara had been employed there for two years, was fully reliable and could help me any time I asked for her assistance. Only on Saturday evening she would go to a movie with her fiancé, but was always home by midnight. "My husband is also here this weekend," Helen continued, "and he too will look after his son. You can call him at the office any time you have a question." No, she was not going hunting all by herself, Lieutenant Hoffman was accompanying her.

My brain was working overtime. "Please, Helen, please consider that your husband isn't all that happy when you go hunting with the young lieutenant; if you do that, he might want to get even and go hunting for me!" She moved toward the door and then turned around. Her high boots, her leather jacket, the rifle over her shoulder made her look so different, like a person I had never seen before. My panic seemed to have reached her, there was a long silence. Then, finally, her answer hit me: "That would be to your liking, wouldn't it! You can forget about that little plan of yours, my marriage can't be destroyed by you, you hear."

"Dearest Helen," I beseeched her, "if I had any such thoughts, would I talk to you about them? In fact, Frank sent me in the cellar the other night to fetch a bottle of wine for dinner, and then he stood in the door and wouldn't let me through; he held me real tight and I pushed him to get out." I blurted it out. "I want you to tell him to leave me be, I am afraid of him."

Now, she was getting angry: "Your imagination is playing tricks on you. I am sure my husband loves only me!" I didn't notice that the situation had anything to do with love. I could not let her go: "I want to go back to my mother; I am not going to stay here!" "Nonsense," said Helen, "your mother hasn't called once since you got here, she is glad we took you in. I think you should get my husband out of your

47

teenage imagination. I know him better than you. He wouldn't dream of cheating on me. It is you who is pushing her luck." She turned around, walked out, and got in the car. The lieutenant was at the wheel, and they drove away.

It was perfectly clear to me that her departure changed my situation to a complete loss. This woman was too dumb and too selfish to even consider the truth. As far as my mother was concerned, my energetic, resourceful, courageous mother was reduced to a slave by this powerful man. The city police were paid off by him once a week, I had noticed in the short time I was at the winery. There was not a chance for me. There was only Klara. Klara was the only person there who had integrity written all over her; the fiancé waited in the entrance hall for her every time he picked her up. She had told me that they planned their wedding for next spring and that she worked to save some money for this joyful occasion. If Klara became my ally, she would lose her job, but she seemed enough of a human being to help me. The maid was my only hope.

That Friday evening after his wife had left and after Klara had gone up to her room in the attic, Frank pushed me on the living-room couch and held me very tight. I jumped up and got a hold of the telephone on the coffee table. "I want to go home," I screamed. "I'll tell my mother to come and get me!"

A malicious smile told me that I was confronting a dangerous predator. "Your mother will come to take you home, will she? Your mother can't even take a streetcar, let alone a train! Your mother is going to a concentration camp the day I don't help her again! You need to stop your annoying delusions!" He let out a sardonic laugh, as if he was pleased with his speech. Then, he got up as if he were deeply offended, left the room, and slammed the door.

Thank God he was gone! I drank the rest of the bottle of

wine that was still on the coffee table in the hopes that this would help me to recover from the shock. When I was sure that he was nowhere around, I tiptoed over to the huge kitchen and fixed the baby's bottle for the night. The kitchen was immaculately clean. Klara was doing a tremendous job as a maid; I felt so much better in her domain. How I envied her and her clean and orderly life! *It is still possible that he is discouraged by my total lack of enthusiasm. If I remain defensive, maybe he'll give up trying.*

After I had changed and fed the little fellow, I put him in the crib next to me and we both went to sleep. In my deepest sleep, I felt something heavy falling on top of me. I had forgotten that there were three doors in this large room and none of them had a key in the lock. "You are hurting me!" I managed to mumble. He put his hand over my mouth: "If you make one more sound, the kid is going to wake up and scream his head off all night." The feeling this scene generated inside me was not pleasant.

My head was someplace else and I kept thinking, *I have underestimated this man, he is quite capable of crudeness, amusing himself in front of his son's crib; he is going to let my mother go to her death and me too.* All he had to do was nothing next time we were in need of help. I thought of the time he had let me go hungry at the hotel in Ravensburg, just because I had refused him. This man worked differently from anybody I had encountered so far. When Frank sneaked out of the room a few minutes later, I said to myself: *Now I know what a Nazi is; they work differently from other people.*

The next day at the lunch table he informed me that he was giving a drinking party to the SS (Hitler's Storm Troopers). "You had best stay upstairs. I don't want any of them to know that I am hiding you at my house; helping Jews is punishable by law, in case you didn't know." I had not thought about that. I had to admit, he didn't mind taking chances. At suppertime, I picked up some food in the kitchen. Klara told me that her fiancé was waiting and that she would go to the show with him. "I'll be back around midnight," she said. "Klara, I envy you." It was all I could mumble, but her response was startling: "That I can believe," she stated quietly. Something inside me said triumphantly "She knows all about it, I have an accomplice! I am not all alone any more!"

I stayed upstairs while the noise downstairs got louder and louder. I didn't have any idea how many people were roughhousing down there, but some of them came upstairs to use the bathroom. They were running around to find it and since there was no key in my doors, I went to bed early, turned off all the lights, and listened to the goings-on downstairs.

There was a thumping sound and then loud laughter; they must be jumping off of something. Even if one should stumble into my room, they would surely assume that I was the maid. "I wish I were the maid, I have sunk so low that I wish I were the maid." I thought of Mother and that she could have called at least once by now and I cried bitterly. Between two or three in the morning, the noise died down and I was able to sleep.

Helen was back Sunday night, bright-eyed and rosy-cheeked. Life went on as if nothing had happened; as if everyone was perfectly satisfied with the situation. Frank was an attentive husband and a loving father, and he raped me down in the wine cellar, where he sent me to work, turning bottles of champagne. His wife didn't notice anything out of order, she tried to be nice to me, bought little gifts for me, an alarm clock, a comb and brush set, but avoided talking to me. My mother didn't call once, Frank had been right there. She was glad to be rid of me. She did not miss me.

Klara was busy preparing her wedding; she was a kind

of mirror, where I could see the distorted ugliness of my situation. I was constantly looking for a way out, but there didn't seem to be one. Mother was living at the Beckers' house in Munich and she did not have to pay rent, probably because she couldn't. Maybe she did not have the money to make long-distance phone calls.

Actually, I didn't know that she still lived there; with Gert not at home, she could have been deported. I worried so much and did not realize that these were only storm clouds gathering, the thunderbolt would hit me a little later.

Shortly before Christmas, two things happened simultaneously: The Beckers gave a big Christmas party for the local Gestapo, and I had missed my period. It felt as if hot oil were poured over me every time I thought about it. On the day of the festivity, Helen told me to pack my things and move up to the attic. I had never been up there and was surprised to find a studio apartment, complete with bath and a small kitchen. Helen said she would have to keep the door locked because the Gestapo would be all over the lower floor. Klara, Helen said, would have a key also and would take good care of me.

"What about your baby? Don't I have to look after Johann?" "Not any more," she said. "I don't want you around my child any more." "Why not?" I demanded. "Well, we are leaving to go up north to the lower Rhine to pay my sister Anna a Christmas visit. We are taking Johann with us, because we'll be gone the whole week. You are to stay up here, because the Gestapo has us under surveillance. Don't make any phone calls and don't go out. Klara will bring you good food every day; she has the key, and you can trust her."

My God, what was happening now? Could it be that Beckers are giving a party because the Gestapo is getting suspicious of them? Or did Frank talk to his wife about me and she reacted by getting him out of there to see her sister. The total lack of sympathy for me would indicate that she was really mad at me, but wanted to gain time.

What was I to do up there in the attic? Was it going to be a whole week, maybe more? Was Klara going to hold me prisoner up there? Could I talk her into letting me leave and go back home while the Beckers were gone? I did not have any money, not a penny, and from Karlsruhe to Munich was a three-hour train ride; from here to Karlsruhe was an hour ride, and I would have to change trains at Karlsruhe. Yes, Karlsruhe was also the place where Frank was going to take me to a lady he knew, if I got pregnant; she was probably a quack, practicing medicine without a license, abortions only!

After a restless night in my new studio, the cars were roaring up and down the driveway all night, I felt absolutely miserable. I missed the baby already, little Johann was now on the way to the lower Rhine country; I had been there once as a six-year-old and remembered how peaceful it had been at the big house that was Anna's inheritance. Both sisters, Anna and Helen, had lost their parents early.

On the second day of my banishment in the attic, I took out a pen and paper and wrote down my confused thoughts. Strangely enough I felt sorry for Helen with her lying, cheating husband. The only person I hated from the depth of my heart was Frank. Some day in the future, I hoped I could have my revenge! I wrote myself into a deep depression. I needed to find a way out.

I cornered Klara on the third day of my imprisonment. I implored her to let me go. I needed to see my mother; she was all alone in Munich. I would head for home, if she could lend me a little money. She said she would have to think about it, but she added that she would need the Beckers' employment until spring. She was not sure it was the right thing to let me leave, since I was only sixteen and not yet considered an adult.

The next morning, she left my breakfast at the table inside the door and did not wake me. I could no longer face the day by myself, with my period still missing. I ran around in continuous circles, went through my few possessions, and found a sleeping pill in my toilet bag. My mother always gave me a sleeping pill when I could not sleep; Dr. Zanders had given those to her on account of our situation. It was strong enough to put me out of my misery for the day. Klara left both the lunch and supper by the door.

It was Saturday, she was going to be gone until midnight. I was so sorry that I had to be awake, and I wanted to go back to sleep. The idea of going to sleep forever seemed attractive to me. I would not have to fear any longer that Frank could take me to Karlsruhe to that woman and her miserable trade. I had only that evening when Klara was gone until midnight. It was Christmastime, and I decided to end my life; to bring a child into this world that would, like me, not have a father, seemed by far the greater misfortune. The kitchenette of the studio had a gas stove. I turned on the oven and the gas came out freely. I had to act before Klara would be back. I wanted to be with my father in heaven, and I made sure that I wouldn't fail in rescuing myself.

At approximately eight o'clock, I took the feather pillow from my bed and fastened it behind my neck. I thought once more of calling my mother, but that would not be any relief from my pain. Then I remembered a little verse from my childhood. It had frightened me when I was still very young, maybe four years old:

> Dorla-girl, Dorla-girl—nobody ever wanted her . . .
> Came the cook, the girl he took
> Put her in the oven,

And then in the coffin.

I turned on the gas, put my head into the oven with the pillow covering the opening behind me. *God, forgive me, but I cannot face Frank Becker again and he will not drive me to the person in Karlsruhe.* Very quickly, I lost consciousness.

On this very Saturday, Klara came home exceptionally early. The movie was sold out and she didn't feel like going anywhere else. She was home at 9:30 and smelled the gas immediately. She turned it off and called the Beckers at her sister's place. She told me later that Helen said they were leaving to drive back, that no doctor was to be called.

An excruciating flash of pain in my head awakened me from unconsciousness. I drifted off again and again; the piercing pain was joined by more upheaval in my lower abdomen, more pain. Helen sat by my bed and shoved small pieces of ice in my mouth. Klara came in to bring something to eat, but I could not swallow because my tongue and throat were swollen. Klara said loud and clear: "Somebody needs to call a doctor!" But nobody showed up. The pain in my head and in my stomach got worse. Helen was there every time I woke from my delirious blackout. I broke out into sweat, and a big clot passed into the bed. My body was a separate thing, did not belong to me. I was merely watching it when it produced more blood.

Helen put an ice bag on my head. "Is it getting better?" she asked. "No, it isn't getting better, but I can't feel it because I'm dead." "You are losing a lot of blood, but you are not dead." She seemed concerned. "I think you just got your period back and will get well soon." *Does that remark mean she got it?* She continued: "When you are completely well, I will send you home to your mother." "What about Johann?" "I don't want you around my child any more, I'll hire a nurse. You are not a stable person, and you are making a lot

54

of trouble for me. Klara is involved too, well, she is leaving next spring anyway."

Her words were music to me. I prayed: "Dear God, you have heard my desperate cries. I am leaving the Becker world. I am ready for a new and different life." My sleep became peaceful, grateful.

I don't know how long it took, but I left as soon as I was strong enough; I never saw Frank again, or Johann. Helen took me to the train station at Karlsruhe, bought my ticket, and said a few bitter words of good-bye: "You messed up my well-meant plans yourself, serves you right that you don't have a job now. Just remember that! If anybody has a second Becker child, it is going to be me, not you!" I didn't listen to her tirade; what flickered through ten layers of irony, was that her rich husband admitted he was "not an angel" and that they restored their Catholic marriage on the spot! When the train pulled out of the station, I was breathing freely.

One hour later, when we were approaching Stuttgart, everyone was ordered off the train. The tracks toward Munich had been destroyed by a bomb, one of the first as far as I knew. We were taken by bus either into town or near the Autobahn, the freeway that Hitler had built in preparation for his war. I had no money to stay overnight, so I walked up to the highway to hitchhike. I was not afraid; I'd found out that I could take care of myself.

Down the dark Autobahn I saw a column of tanks approaching. Machine after heavy machine rolled by me, probably on the way to the front. Suddenly, one of the tanks stopped right in front of me and a voice called out: "You can ride with us, we are going through Munich." I did hesitate; a bunch of young soldiers would be risky for me to join. Since I didn't know who would stop for me next, a criminal or another kind of fiend, I decided to take a smaller chance with the soldiers. I'll just let them talk; words don't hurt me anymore!

Actually, there was not one question being asked, not one word was spoken; it was very noisy and dark inside the machine. I imagined that the six or seven soldiers knew what was waiting for them at the front; maybe they were tired like I was. When I jumped out of the tank, I was near the West Cemetery, and I carried my heavy suitcase all the way to the townhouse, where Mother was waiting for me.

I didn't have the words for it. I was wondering what the Beckers had told Mother about my return home. I soon found out. I was sobbing, stammering, and embracing my mother, when she pushed me away: "When will you grow up, girl? Everybody puts themselves out for you and what do you do but get homesick!" I did not want to be all alone with my recent experience for the rest of my life. I tried to tell my mother so she would understand. Her reaction was startling: "I do not want to know what you did! When you commit a crime, you do not get my sympathy! Stop this hysterical scene and lead a better life!"

Did she say something about a crime? She had given me the word I was looking for. "When Hitler has lost this war, we should sue the Beckers for crimes against underage youth." I blurted it out. I wanted my mother to know! "For God's sake, child, pull yourself together or get out of here! The Beckers are my friends, you hear, my friends! Moreover, when I look at you, I think that it ended quite well at Beckers' house, it could have been worse."

I would never say that it could have been worse and that it ended quite well! I saw my mother in a new way, actually she was not Mother any more, she was a thoroughly frightened individual, who would agree to anything for a small advantage. I had lost my mother and I felt very cold inside. It was obvious that the Nazis were at the base of the entire situation, but for some reason—I didn't know why—I had lost my mother just the same. I was only sixteen and not mature enough to understand.

Also, what I didn't know at the time was the intensified persecution of Jews that had taken effect while I was away. The establishment of the various concentration camps had taken place in the spring of 1940. The National Socialist Party's Office of Racial Identity (*das Rassen-politische Amt der NSDAP*) published the following guidelines on October 14, 1940: "All files on Jews and half-Jews are to be completed and sent to Cologne, giving easy access to Jewish and half-Jewish persons. Our decision is valuable because these people are not of German blood. (*Deutschblutig.*) For that reason the Race-political Office of Cologne is preparing a debasement for all Jews and half-Jews as soon as the war is won."

Mother had been informed of this and—as usual—she didn't talk about it. We believed that Hitler would lose the war, but he hadn't lost it yet! The threat had grown ever more dangerous; it had changed my mother in fundamental ways. This was not the mother I had known, but I made a firm decision to be very good to her and help her all I could. "Have you heard from Gert?" I changed the subject, never to mention it directly again to anybody for the rest of my life! She showed me the letters from France.

When we held the paper up to a light, pinholes appeared under certain letters. Put together, they spelled "All is well in Ostende." His unit was not allowed to disclose information on their location, but he had told us both to hold all his letters close to a light. Where did he take his ideas from? It was characteristic of him that he always outsmarted the system. We didn't hear from him for a long time after that.

I tried to keep busy, helping around the house. We were

still renting out rooms, we but had to be more careful whom we took in. From time to time, I rode my bike down the Isar Valley south of Munich to visit a place where we had spent vacations when our father was still with us. The farmers in Bayerbrunn gave me food and clothes. I was always hungry and groceries were getting scarce.

14. Deferment and Complications

In the spring of 1941, Gert came home. We were overjoyed to see him, but anxious to find out why he was sent home. Mother was worried that it had to do with our "situation." "Yes—" Gert was laughing—"it had to do with *one* of our situations." At the command post, somebody had looked through Gert's file and discovered . . . not his ancestry, but the fact that his mother was a war widow. Only sons of a casualty of war were to serve in their hometown, in a limited capacity. Gert's superior officer quoted the law: "You can go home; you are the only son of a dead soldier." Anybody else would have been grateful, but not Gert. "They are wrecking my plan! If I can't get to the front, I can't protect my family. I'll have to find another way to trick them." Briefly after that came proof that he was right.

In our mailbox lay the first order for deportation of Sara Leonie Gundersheimer to an undisclosed location. This document deserves special explanation. A certified copy is in the Document section. The translation will testify to the nature and insidious intent of the attack on innocent people. It was state-sanctioned robbery and a thinly disguised death threat. Anyone who found this atrocity in their mailbox would consider going into hiding, fleeing the country or, quite often, committing suicide.

The language on the two pages was overbearing and commanding: "Any attempt to evade or resist the deportation will be punished with the strongest State Police measures. Any person who helps the transport participant to escape will be subject to the same punishment as the participant (as if they were participating in some kind of outing). It is mandatory that every transport participant takes along a backpack or small suitcase, 150–200 German marks, complete clothing, appropriate shoes, one blanket, one bowl or pot, one spoon. Knives and forks are not allowed." (Those could be used for self-defense.) "Provisions for a three-day trip are to be carried in a handbag."

My first thought was "How long does one live with one spoon? Why provisions for three days? Can't they stop for meals?" The second page was titled "Jurisdiction Concerning Properties."

All assets, properties and capital of the transport participant are confiscated herewith. Any attempt to displace or hide anything will be followed by the sharpest persecution. All entries on this questionnaire are to be made in clear handwriting in ink. All entries that are incorrect or sloppy, will be taken as an attempt to cheat and will be punished accordingly. The appropriate original papers, mortgages, annuities, savings accounts, bank accounts, insurance contracts, etc., are to be available in a self-addressed envelope and handed to the transport leader at the time of deportation. No valuables can be taken, except for wedding rings. Typewriters, cameras, binoculars and bicycles are to be left in the residence. All of the above mentioned items are to be handed over to the Gestapo officials in charge. All declarations will be thoroughly investigated and verified before departure of the transport (see Document section for the original, German text).

To make sure that everything was executed in a proper and correct way, the transport order was signed and stamped. Three different signatures confirm the correctness of these official statements: Pfeuffer, Angest, and Schmid.

During the three years between 1942 and 1945, we received six such transport orders, one every six months. Each time our reaction was paralyzing fear. It was so nerve-wracking that we were not capable of rational thought. That the death-train would leave without us was each time very unlikely. How did we mange to escape such a sealed fate six times?

We learned much later, after the war, that these transports left at dawn of the same day the participants had been gathered together. In other words, no plan had been made to house or feed these victims. Also of importance was to foil inquiry by neighbors or friends, and to avoid phone calls or written messages. Our frantic schemes to postpone the departure by a few hours worked each time; I am not sure why. The only explanation I have been able to give so far was an enormous amount of just plain luck.

15.   The Volunteer

Close to a thousand people were forced to join the first transport in November of 1941. This was the first of many trains that would go east without any location disclosed. We heard about it from a Herr Markuse, whose girlfriend "Baby" had been taken away, never to return. I shuddered. The thought of such a train left me sleepless many a night. Trains give me an uneasy feeling to this very day. I could not mention my depression to anyone, but I felt it was only a matter of time until "they" would catch up with us. My brother Gert was already a step ahead of such a development.

After he had been dismissed, as the only son of a war-widow, he brooded a short time, and then decided that he needed to volunteer for the Russian front. He needed to be ahead of the Gestapo. The commander had never experienced such enthusiasm for the war; Gert had to sign two questionnaires: one that he was volunteering and proceeding at his own risk, a second one that he was of pure Aryan descent; another death threat was attached to this paper, aimed at anyone who gave false information.

Gert gave false information; the Russian front itself was another death threat! He didn't usually talk about his adventures, but he showed me this questionnaire proudly. In an unobserved moment at the commander's office, he had removed it from his application packet and nobody noticed it was missing. They were so impressed with his willingness to "do something meaningful" that they made him a lieutenant! During the first few days in November, we took him to the train that would take him into the Russian winter; another death train! "Send a telegram if anything bad happens," he said. "I will handle our affairs from the war zone, and that will confuse them to no end."

My brother never talked about the time he spent in combat on the Crimean Peninsula; he mentioned that he led a successful retreat when they had too many casualties; he was praised for that, to his greatest amazement! Between battles, he wrote the letters to the families of the fallen heroes. Suddenly, he was sent home on furlough because "his mother was dying." When he arrived at home in his filthy, torn, spotted uniform, tired out by the long journey, we gave him the transport order we had received. Gert stood up, asked me to have something hot to drink for him when he would be back, and gone he was.

Gert went straight to the Gestapo headquarters, busted into the office for "Jewish Affairs," and hollered; "How nice and warm you have it here in your comfortable office! I bring you greetings from the front in Russia, where we are all freezing to death! I am going back there tomorrow, and I expect you to leave my family alone with your deportation threats!" The scene filled him with a certain satisfaction, and he played it out to the fullest. "Consider," he continued, "that we don't have time for your racial theories! If you bother me again, I will let the commando of our armed forces handle the matter! This time I came here myself to spare you the embarrassment, do you understand?"

They were stunned; they obviously had never encountered such a situation before; they were at a loss and did not know what to do. Someone whose life in Germany was made into a nightmare had gone to the Russian front in the winter. Why does he fight for a Fatherland that wants to destroy him? Finally they decided to remove our entire file from the active to the inactive drawer. They preferred not to mess with the armed forces in time of war.

Gert was not convinced. His strategy had worked as planned and he should have been happy, but he muttered: "I know these cowards all too well, I'm afraid they'll get rid of me."

After returning to his outfit at the Russian front, he got notice that he was relieved of his term of duty, dismissed because of his racial background (see Document section). Six times, the Gestapo sent us the transport order, to an undisclosed location in the East. Each time we fooled them, our desperate plan succeeded, but we knew it would only work one time. After they discovered how we tricked them, they would be back with greater precision and we had best be prepared with a different answer. . . .

Lonny Gundersheimer and Wilhelm van Laak became engaged in 1917, during the First World War.

Lonny was a Red Cross nurse and worked in a veteran's hospital during the First World War.

Lonny and her children in 1928

Sister and brother in 1930

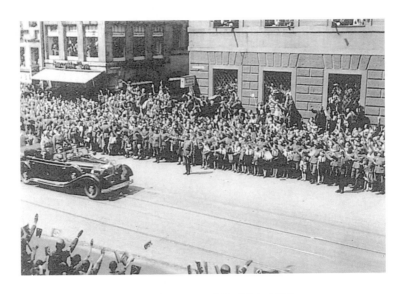

Hitler on the streets of Munich in 1934

Lieutenant of the Reserve Wilhelm van Laak, holder of the Iron Cross, died at age 44 as a result of his injuries in World War I.

An den Folgen schwerer Kriegsverletzungen verschied Dienstag abend nach langem Krankenlager mein inniggeliebter Mann, der treusorgende Vater seiner Kinder

Herr Wilhelm van Laak
Kaufmann

Oberleutnant der Reserve, Inhaber des Eisernen Kreuzes, im Alter von 44 Jahren.

München, Birkenleiten 15, 11. April 1935

In tiefster Trauer: Lonny van Laak
*16182;   mit Kindern Gerhard und Dorothea

Die Beisetzung findet am Freitag, 12. April, vorm. 10 Uhr, in Ebenhausen-Zell (Isartal) mit darauffolgendem Trauergottesdienst statt.

At the convent school, Günzburg, in May 1935

Topsy in Father's big chair

With my best friend Christine, summer of 1935

Hitler visited Munich, Kaufingerstrasse, on the occasion of the
Czechoslovakian crisis in 1938.

Mother, Gert, and Dorla just before World War II
in 1939

Grandmother's passport photo when she had to leave Germany. She died in Paraguay in 1948.

My brother Gert leaving for the Russian front during the first year of the Second World War.

Mother took this picture on my reaction to the new law that
stated that Jews are to be removed from public transportation and all recreational facilities, including the swimming pool "Dantebad."

Our underground shelter, where
we spent entire nights during
heavy bombardment of Munich.
Seventy-five percent of the city
was destroyed, including the city
block of Gestapo headquarters
on Brienner Street.

Dr. med. Theodor Zanders
verstorben am 4. September 1946

In unvergeßlicher Liebe

Dr. Theodore Zanders, our physician who gave us medical care and medicine through twelve years of terror and Nazi persecution.

Name, Vorname, Dienstgrad, Dienststellung und Verlheinhungstag
Truppentiel

bei der Verleihung   Hölz, Hans Hptm.,
Kdt. Z. Gen. Stabsausbildg.   Beim VI. A.K. Fhr. E. Kampfgr.
Awarded 23.2.44   Died +26.12.43

Captain Hans Hölz, who received the Knight's Cross for breaking out of en-
circlement on December 26, 1943. He died that day during an attempt to
save his training unit.

Dorothea Wieck, who grew up at my parents' house and became famous for her avant-garde movie *Mädchen in Uniform*. She provided my brother a connection to the German counter-intelligence service when all his efforts to save his family had failed in the Spring of 1944.

München, den *9.* Juli 19*38*

Unterschrift der Eltern: Das Direktorat: Die Leiter in der Klasse:

Winterzeugnis

Betragen	Fleiß	Leibeserziehung	Deutschkunde				Naturwissenschaften und Mathematik				Fächer des Frauenschaffens					Fremdsprachen			Religionslehre	
			Deutsch	Geschichte	Erdkunde	Kunsterziehung	Musik	Biologie	Chemie	Physik	Rechnen und Mathematik	Kochen	Haus- und Gartenarbeit	Handarbeit	Pflege-Gesundheitslehre und -pflege	Beschäftigungslehre	Englisch	Französisch	Latein	
										—		—						—		

Bemerkungen: *die Aufstellung eines Nichtzeugnisses ist wegen der dau-*
ernden Abwesenheit der Schülerin unmöglich.

München, den *11.* Dezember 19*38*

Unterschrift der Eltern: Das Direktorat: Die Leiter in der Klasse:

München, den *6.* Juli 19*39*

Unterschrift der Eltern: Das Direktorat: Die Leiterin der Klasse:

Winterzeugnis

Betragen	Fleiß	Leibeserziehung	Deutschkunde				Naturwissenschaften und Mathematik				Fächer des Frauenschaffens					Fremdsprachen			Religionslehre
			Deutsch	Geschichte	Erdkunde	Kunsterziehung	Musik	Biologie	Chemie	Physik	Rechnen und Mathematik	Kochen	Haus- und Gartenarbeit	Handarbeit	Pflege-Gesundheitslehre und -pflege	Beschäftigungslehre	Englisch	Französisch	Latein
2	2	—	2	1	2	—	1	2	2	—	4	3		2			2		1

Bemerkungen: *Es ist sehr zu beanstanden, daß die Schülerin bei der*
ohnehin sehr verkürzten Unterrichtszeit so viele Versäumnis-
se aufzuweisen hat.

Leistungsstufen:

1 = sehr gut
2 = gut
3 = befriedigend
4 = ausreichend
5 = mangelhaft
6 = ungenügend

Notenstufen: 1 = sehr gut, 2 = gut, 3 = genügend, 4 = nicht genügend.

München, den *21.* Dezember 19*39*

Das Direktorat: Die Leiterin der Klasse:

Unterschrift der Eltern:

Nr. 1601. Verlag J. Maiß, München, Herrnstr. 8   ~ 162 ~   68

Two grade reports from July 6 and December 21, 1938. Two teachers state that the student was absent most of the time during the 1938–39 school year. After that, no school could accept students who did not have proof of Aryan descent.

A b s c h r i f t

Der Beauftragte des Gauleiters
für Arisierung

München 22, den 14. Okt. 1941
Widenmayerstraße 27
Rufnummer 25231/28811

An den
Herrn Oberbürgermeister der
Hauptstadt der Bewegung,
Reichsleiter Karl F i e h l e r

M ü n c h e n

Betreff: Benutzung der städt. Straßenbahnen und Omnibusse
durch Juden.

Sehr geehrter Herr Oberbürgermeister!

Der Gauleiter und Herr Staatsminister Adolf WAGNER hat, in seiner
Eigenschaft als Reichsverteidigungskommissar, zur Aufrechterhaltung der
Ruhe und Ordnung gestern die Anordnung gegeben, dass den Juden das Be-
nutzen der städtischen Verkehrsmittel mit sofortiger Wirksamkeit verboten
ist.
Die Israelitische Kultusgemeinde München habe ich angewiesen, ihre Mit-
glieder von diesem Verbot in Kenntnis zu setzen.
Ich bitte um gefl. Kenntnisnahme.

Besuch des Tierparks Hellabrunn durch Juden:

Aus Kreisen der Bevölkerung sind bei der Kreisleitung der NSDAP. Be-
schwerden eingegangen, dass die Juden sich Sonntags nach wie vor im
Tierpark Hellabrunn aufhalten. Im Einvernehmen mit Kreisleiter Pg.
LEDERER darf ich Ihnen die Bitte unterbreiten, die Tierparkverwaltung
Hellabrunn anzuweisen, künftighin die Juden aus den Anlagen des Tier-
parks zu entfernen.

Heil Hitler !
gez. Wegner
(Wegner) .

SA-Hauptsturmführer.

Quelle: Yad Vashem MRP-2/1

By ordinance of the minister of State, Adolf Hitler, Jews are forbidden to
use public transportation or to enter public parks like the zoo; they are to
be removed from said locations as of today.

Oberkommando der Wehrmacht   Berlin, den /. April 1943
Az. 1 1 20.12 AWA/J IVEII (If)
Nr. 11 143/43

                                                    Einschreiben
                              Herrn

                              Gerhard van L a a k
                                   M ü n c h e n 19
                                   Hofenfelsstr. 54

    Auf Ihr Gesuch vom 17.11.42 teilt Ihnen das Oberkommando der
Wehrmacht mit, daß Ihre KINWEIBUNG – Wiedereinberufung – zum
aktiven Wehrdienst nach den geltenden Bestimmungen nicht möglich ist.

                         Der Chef des Oberkommandos der Wehrmacht
                                  Im Auftrage

                                    [signature]

. .4 Anlagen

My brother Gert's false papers and other tricks he used to wear the uniform
of the Armed Forces—in order to protect the three of us from the brutal attacks of the Gestapo—fell in like a house of cards when this letter dismissed him under ordinance of the present-day restrictions.

Geheime Staatspolizei
Staatspolizeileitstelle München
B.Nr.   II G/Kra.

München, den 7. Januar 1940

An

    Leonie Sara van L a a k , geb. Gundersheim

                M ü n c h e n
                Hofenfelsstr.54.

Betrifft: Abwanderung

Anlagen: 1 Vermögenserklärung

I.

Sie werden davon verständigt, dass Sie zu einem Abwanderungstransport
eingeteilt sind.

Sie haben sich ab 12.1.40 in Ihrer jetzigen Unterkunft bereitzuhalten
und dürfen diese ohne Erlaubnis der Geheimen Staatspolizei - Staatspolizeileitstelle München nicht - auch nicht vorübergehend - verlassen.

Jeder Versuch, sich der Abwanderung zu widersetzen oder zu entziehen,
wird mit strengsten staatspolizeilichen Massnahmen geahndet.

Jeder Transportteilnehmer darf als Gepäck nur einen Handkoffer oder
einen Rucksack mitnehmen. Sperriges Gut darf nicht mitgenommen werden.

Es muss pro Person mitgenommen werden: 150 bis 200 M,
vollständige Bekleidung (ordentliches Schuhwerk), Bettzeug mit Decke,
Essgeschirr (Teller oder Topf) mit Löffel. Messer und Gabeln dürfen
nicht mitgenommen werden.

Die Verpflegung während des Transportes für 3 Tage ist mitzubringen.
Dieser Reiseproviant kann in einer Handtasche mitgeführt werden.

II.

In vermögensrechtlicher Hinsicht ergeht folgende staatspolizeiliche Ver-
fügung:

Das gesamte Vermögen der zur Abwanderung eingeteilten vorstehend genann-
ten Juden wird mit Rückwirkung vom ....1940 staatspolizeilich beschlag-
nahmt. Jeder Versuch einer Vermögensverschiebung oder Hinterziehung
wird sofort mit schärfsten staatspolizeilichen Massnahmen geahndet.

Anliegende Vermögenserklärung ist genauestens auszufüllen und hand-
schriftlich zu unterzeichnen. Die Eintragungen haben in deutlicher
Handschrift zu erfolgen. Vermögenserklärungen, die unrichtig, nach-
lässig oder undeutlich ausgefüllt sind, werden als Versuchte Vermö-
genshinterziehung behandelt und deren Fertiger, wie angedroht, be-
straft. Die Vermögenserklärungen werden noch <u>vor</u> dem Abtransport in
allen Einzelheiten nachgeprüft.

Bereitzuhalten sind sämtliche in die Vermögenserklärung aufzunehmende
und das Vermögen verkörpernde Urkunden, wie Wertpapiere, Sparkassen-
bücher, Hypothekenurkunden, Lebensversicherungspolicen usw. soweit
diese nicht laut abgegebener Erklärung anderweitig verwahrt sind. Dies
Urkunden sind in einem geeigneten Umschlag mit Aufschrift der genauen
Personalien des Inhabers gesammelt zu verwahren.

Bereitzuhalten sind weiter ebenfalls nicht mitzunehmende Wertgegen-
stände und Wertsachen jeder Art, wie Schmuck, Gold, Silber, Platin usw
mit Ausnahme des Eheringes.

Schreibmaschinen, Fotoapparate, Ferngläser und Fahrräder sind in der
Wohnung zu belassen und in die Vermögenserklärung aufzunehmen.

Die weisungsgemäss ausgefertigte Vermögenserklärung ist mit sämtlichen
bereitzuhaltenden Papieren und Gegenständen dem einfordernden Beamten
bei Abholung auszufolgen.

I.A.
gez.Pfeuffer

Für die Richtigkeit:
gez.Schmid
Verw.Angest.
(Dienstsiegel)

This is.acertified true copy:

GORDON W. ROSS
Captain, Sig C
Commanding, Munich
Detachment, 6870th DISCC

Every six months, the Gestapo sent a two-page letter to the "Transport Participants," informing them in detail of the immediate deportation to an undisclosed location.

Geburtsurkunde

(Auszug aus dem beim Amtsgericht _____B u c h e n_____ verwahrten

Geburtsbuch der _israelitischen_ Gemeinde _Hainstadt_

vom Jahre _1830_)

Nach dem Eintrag auf Seite _50_ Nr. _14_ wurde am

siebenten Dezember

des Jahres eintausendachthundert _dreißig_

zu _Hainstadt_ **geboren**

xxxxxxxxxxxxxxxxxxxxxxxxxxxxxxxxxxxxxxxxxxxxxxxxxxxxx jakob 2

Inseln, Sohn des Faist guntersheimer, Schutzbürgers

und Weinwirtes dahier, und der Karolina, geborenen

Killin von Eirheim.

Für die Richtigkeit des Auszugs

Buchen den _31. Oktober_ 19_39_.

Der Urkundsbeamte der Geschäftsstelle:

Huber

Justizinspektor

Gebühr: _0,60 RM._

Geburtsurkunde

— 168 —

This is a copy of one document the Gestapo used to systematically ruin and destroy us: the birth certificate of our great-grandfather, from the year 1830. It was obtained from the Israeli community in the county of Hainstadt, registered at the courthouse in the town of Buchen. This and other documents of that nature were our only "crime." They were in the files of Gestapo headquarters in Munich and were the basis for the twice-yearly order of deportation to a concentration camp.

Theodor Israel Koronczyk   ..ünchen, Datum des Poststempels
      Vertrauensmann
der Reichsvereinigung der Juden
      in Deutschland

     M ü n c h e n 13
  Isabellastrasse 56/1
  Telefon 37 20 54

            V o r l a d u n g

Der Herr Beauftragte des Gauleiters hält am **12. Mai 1944**
im Anwesen der ehemaligen Bezirksstelle, Lindwurmstrasse 125 Rckg.
Erdgeschoss, um 1/2 7 Uhr abends, einen Apell für sämtliche Juden
im Bereich der Stadt München.
Hiezu ist das Erscheinen Aller angeordnet.
Entschuldigungen werden unter keinen Umständen angenommen.
Zur Feststellung der Erschienenen, wird am Eingang Kontrolle gehalten.
Da der Apell pünktlichst beginnt, ist rechtzeitiges Erscheinen unerlässlich, damit bei der Kontrolle keine Stockung eintritt.
Der Apell findet in 4 Abteilungen statt. Ihr Erscheinen wurde für den
oben angegebenen Tag angeordnet.
Sollten Sie um diese Zeit im Arbeitseinsatz stehen, so wollen Sie
diese Vorladung Ihrem Betriebsführer, zwecks zeitweiser Beurlaubung,
vorlegen.

                  Theodor Israel Koronczyk

16.   Bismarck

There was a lot of hearsay going around, and we didn't believe most of that, but I had two sources of information that proved accurate every time. One was my little radio, where I could get the German news program from the BBC in the middle of the night. Often, I stayed up until 2:00 A.M. to hear Vaughn Monroe singing "Racing with the Moon," which was their theme song, I believe. While our schemes to fool the Gestapo were getting more and more reckless, this song struck a chord in me: We too seem to be racing with the moon, or so I thought. The other source of reliable information was my brother Gert. He never told me where he got it, but he knew all kinds of things before everybody else talked about it. It was possible that he had some connections with the student resistance movement at the University of Munich; but that was not "little-girls-stuff" and he never answered my questions.

I don't know where I heard it first: The German battleship *Bismarck* had sunk the pride of the Royal Navy, the flagship *Hood,* on May 24, 1941. Of the 1,400 crew members, only three survived. Of course I could not let anyone know that this bit of news was really troublesome. I was very upset. I remembered my English instructor from the ninth-grade, an Anglophile, telling us about the might of the British Navy. She was one of my dearest teachers, and she put her opinions in terms that ninth-grade girls could understand: "When the British lion awakens from sleep," she would say, "it will lift its mighty paw and smash the German fleet!" We admired her courage, also the way she emphasized her words by banging her fist on the desk. It was impressive!

By the time the triumphant news of the victorious *Bismarck* was all over Germany, I was waiting for the lion to lift its paw. I was still crying for all those young kids who had gone to their eternal rest in the icy waters of the North Atlantic, when the BBC gave the particulars of the sinking of the *Bismarck,* with her 2,200 crew. Only 110 of them had been rescued, because a German U-boat showed up at the battle area, causing the rescuers to flee. Over two thousand had to be left to drown. It was the end of the world as we had known it, just as Father had predicted. How can anyone put a child into this cruel world? I resolved never to do that.

17.   Dorothea

There was more than one agency involved in what the rest of the world has since come to know as "Hitler's solution of the Jewish problem." As soon as one break in the proverbial dam had been stopped, there appeared a few drops somewhere else in the form of an inquiry, now a postcard in our mailbox. I stared at it transfixed; it meant that "they" knew where to contact us. *How do I tell my mother without her falling into her state of suspended animation?* From one minute to the next, on such occasions, she would look twenty years older, white as a sheet, fragile and in need of someone to hold her up. With such a notice in one hand, I answered the telephone with the other.

"You sound positively awful," said a familiar voice. "Are you perhaps letting them get you down? What is the matter with you? No real friend of mine is ever going to sound that bad! Wait until you hear what I have planned for you and Gert and your mother! I want you all to come to the Palace Hotel and have dinner with me tonight! How about it? Yes, it is possible, if you leave your worries at home and the rest up to me. Just hurry up and find something to wear. Let me speak to your darling mother! Just imagine, my little doll, I have an insanely jealous admirer with me here this evening, and I cannot be alone with him. I need you three to give my little party for five, to be safe, you understand?"

Well, of all things! I gave Mother the phone and listened intensely to all her objections. I forgot to give her the notice.

This was Dorothea Wieck, a real movie star. She had earned considerable fame before she was twenty years old. She was just sixteen when she conquered the hearts of people from her stage at the Munich Civic Theater; then came her movie, *Mädchen in Uniform* (Girls in Uniform). She played the leading role of a lesbian teacher in an all-girl school. The film was avant-garde at the time and became a sensation. It netted her a contract in Hollywood, where she spent several years.

When Hitler came to power, she fell into disfavor in Germany because of her success in the United States. After her return to Munich, she was considered a has-been, she was still in her twenties, and she played only small roles from then on. This did not diminish her spirit in any way; her main interest in life seemed to be the men who flocked around her. My mother, who had known Dorothea from childhood on, used to say there was safety in numbers as far as the men in her life were concerned.

I remember when my parents were invited to the villa of Hans Albers, a famous 1930s movie star. Gert and I, still kids, went along to go swimming in Lake Starnberg. Around the dinner table was an assembly of movie stars: The comic Ludwig Schmitz, Albers himself, Adalbert von Schlettow of *Nibelungen* fame (he played the traitor Hagen), and Dorothea, accompanied by my parents. After a lengthy meal, Schlettow insisted we take a walk by the lake. He took Doro by the arm and led her out to the end of the pier, where he picked her up and threw her in the lake. Headfirst he played the life-guard, pulled her back out, and dried her very carefully. We assumed that he did all that in order to get close to Dorothea's famous beauty.

"How are you managing these lousy times?" she wanted to know when we were alone with her in an elegant hotel room. Mother told her that things were getting worse for us. "I don't know how long we can hold out. We had several notices from the Gestapo—and our doctor is not sure that he can keep them satisfied much longer. Last time they were at our place, he could barely convince them to wait because I would die anyway, from a cancerous tumor. All this seems to get increasingly dangerous; I am thinking about disappearing into Switzerland! What else could we do?"

"What else is there?" echoed Dorothea and started biting her carefully lacquered fingernails. "Give me a few days time and keep me posted; in the meantime, I will think of something, believe me, I will think of something fast."

A few days later, she was on the phone: "Could you have a little snack ready for me and a friend tonight? I want you to meet my newest suitor; he is a darling of a man, you will be absolutely crazy about him. He wants to marry me, and I just might do that. He is with the German *Abwehr* (Counter Intelligence)."

"You are out of your mind, Doro! You are getting yourself and us into a whole lot of trouble! This kind of thing is not going to help us, quite the contrary!" Mother was no longer optimistic. "Nonsense," said Dorothea, "you need to meet him first. This man wouldn't hurt a fly, I guarantee it; but I promise you that I'll get rid of him if you don't trust him. I'll drop him as fast as I dropped that other man, remember, at the 'Palace,' if you have any doubts after meeting him; all I'd tell him is that I want him to meet my 'God child' and her mother for one evening, big deal, is it."

We talked it over, the three of us, and we knew her well enough to realize that she just might have her usual success; she was a strange character, very determined and sure of herself. We agreed to go along with her experiment, since she would be careful and trustworthy.

The evening with Dorothea and Georg Neuner was a terrific success. It is difficult to explain that he fell in love with us, and we with him, but that is what happened. The main reason was probably Dorothea's influence; when she was determined to conquer someone's heart, few would resist; least of all Neuner. He was a very quiet man, who pretended that he could not talk on account of a clearly visible injury; he had had quite a bit of plastic surgery done on his face, and behind this mask he could afford to play his games undisturbed, and in silence.

Shortly after dinner (he still had not said one word), he stuck a pipe between two rows of artificial-looking teeth, and began to talk with clenched jaws, drawing big puffs of smoke between each word; he told us that he was a collector of musical instruments of past centuries, that his home looked like a museum, and that he had traveled quite a bit to establish his collection; he was obviously dead-struck by Dorothea's charms, which was understandable considering that Doro was genuinely fond of him. All of us tried the entire evening to make him laugh, and he grimaced for us in a good-natured way. My brother, who had taken up photography lately, took some very nice portraits of him, which pleased him no end.

When they finally left around midnight, we were much impressed and quite sure that this man couldn't kill a fly. Whatever it was he was doing with the Gestapo or Secret Service, we decided, was most definitely a put-on, probably due to the fact that he knew he could get away with it; Doro said that some people he associated with did not know that he could talk; I imagine that he could accomplish a great deal when he never needed to answer to anyone. Dorothea was busy part of the time with making a film, and Georg was soon coming to see us by himself; perhaps he hoped that she would show up, perhaps he was just lonely and enjoyed our company.

It was not long until we could tell him that we were

constantly threatened by police action. He sat there in silence for a long time. Then, drawing heavily on his pipe, he muttered: "Goddamn, I can't do much for you either; all I can do is let you know well in advance when they are planning to come by here, and you are never going to be home when they get here. That's all."

We knew that they avoided any commotion around the neighborhood and figured that, as long as somebody uninvolved would open the door and tell them that we were not home, they would most probably just turn around and come back the next day; if they actually did return within that week, nobody would answer the door, but Luschuwa next door would open a window and tell them that we were gone for several months and that she didn't know where, "just to visit with relatives."

Our only fear was that Neuner would miss out on getting the information just once, but he never did. He was the most conscientious agent anyone could have, meticulous, pedantic, and one hundred percent reliable. He kept us in relative safety for some time, a little bit like his ancient musical instruments, which he also kept from falling apart. After the years of the Reich were finally over, he became director of the city's museum, with a clear record of having stayed in the Secret Service in order to be effective as a humanitarian.

After Doro's film was finished, the day came when she had to leave town. Georg was very sad. He asked us: did we think that she would marry him? Yes, my mother guessed, who knew her the best. "She just might, but I believe that it would not mean a blessed thing." We told him that she had broken many a contract, in Vienna, in Hollywood, in Munich, also in marriage. When she appeared, he asked his heartfelt question. I shall never forget the week that followed. We were all running around in circles with preparations for their wedding. Mother and I went with Neuner to buy a very special wedding gown, size 18, or some such number. I was so impressed with it, seldom had I seen a truly elegant and expensive dress. He bought food and drink for the celebration and my brother took pictures of them and enlarged them himself.

When the evening before the event had finally arrived, Georg Neuner rang our doorbell and asked us to read the letter that she had left for him. We were just a bit frightened then, just for a moment. What would his reaction be now? The four of us sat around the table with Doro's letter and Georg was close to tears. For a while he smoked his pipe in silence, then he said, "I shall need the three of you more than ever now, because I have a wedding dress and no bride. I am a very frugal man and I expect you to help me find a wife who wears a size eighteen dress and who is as lovely as Dorothea, that will not be easy."

Many, many years latter, we went to his wedding. He married a wonderful and beautiful young woman, and both stayed our friends. I don't think it is important, but she did wear that dress.

18.   Swastika Cookies

For a long time, the people of our city were convinced that they had been spared from air attack. There were rumors circulating among our friends that too many RAF pilots had at one time been students in our lovely town and refused, in memory of the good times, to attack it. After all, many northern cities that had been leveled to ashes did not have that record of summer study programs and hospitality. In the beginning of October 1943, these hopes and speculations were eradicated, together with the entire south and east part of the city.

We had dug ourselves a shelter in the backyard, much like a trench. My brother knew something about that from his army days; he made it narrow and curved for added chances of survival and he covered it with heavy logs and a heap of broken cement from bombed buildings. It was a veritable fortress, and we spent our nights there. We outfitted it with electric wiring, which meant we had a little heat and a radio.

Our part of town, near the West Cemetery, was never totally destroyed, as were other parts of the city. Our greatest worry was the municipal natural-gas plant close by, and one night in March of 1943, we were delivered from this threat in the course of an especially heavy bombing attack. The whole "*Gaskessel*" went up with a mild thud and aside from a few broken windows, not much harm was done. During that summer we had an ambitious chicken, sitting on a bunch of eggs, and since the traffic through the garden and basement was constant because of air raids, we had moved her to the attic, where no one else particularly wanted to be during these weeks. She had food and water there and all the peace and quiet she required, and we were hoping for a great number of little chickens, which we dearly needed. During the night the gas plant had exploded, we raced upstairs to see how she had survived.

Amidst a heap of broken glass from the shattered windows sat the mother hen, and all her eggs had broken from the air pressure. Like a miracle in the wake of destruction, all our chickens had hatched at once, while they usually come out of the shell one by one; these were ready, fuzzy, yellow, and all done, the three of us stood there in the attic, full of admiration for the miracle of life before us. We were laughing and crying at once, and then we swept up all the broken glass and continued daily existence without windows and without our gas kitchen stove.

There was no measure taken by the city to replace the natural gas supply, and we had to find some long-term solution to the problem of cooking and heating water. After a tough and hungry time of feeding the family from one electric hot plate, some friends of ours installed a nice-sized wood stove in our kitchen in place of the gas facility; it even had a marvelous little oven. Soon it became known in the neighborhood that one could bake whatever one had to bake at our house. I remember that the Christmas season following some air attacks, brought us a very special situation that nobody with any sense of history could ever forget.

Frau Fruhlich, our SS neighbor's charming wife, had been blessed with raw materials to bake cookies for her four children; she called them "Ferkelchen," or piglets. She must have heard somewhere that we had a woodstove with an oven—and right next door too! She rang our doorbell one evening and asked to use our oven.

It was Christmastime and four children were eager to taste a sample of the season's baking, a rare treat that winter. Maybe she would let us have a taste for the use of our oven? We asked her in, hoping for the best. I was shaking in my shoes. She said the dough was ready, her children were busy cutting out the cookies, and could she be back in an hour to bake them? We fired up the wood stove and when she came back with her precious fare, I joined her in the kitchen and offered to help, a task that Mother avoided taking on.

There she was, chatting amiably, showing me proudly four baking sheets full of cookies in the shapes of swastikas. Big, delicious, slowly rising swastikas were baking in our oven. I hastened back to Mother, who was lying on her couch as usual. I managed to blurt out, "Dozens of swastika-cookies are rising in our oven!"

My mother looked puzzled, and after a long silence, she said; "Those cookies are made with ordinary dough; if the oven doesn't explode, there is nothing I intend to do about it. Leave her alone." *Mahlzeit, bon appetit! Fruhliche Weihnachten.*

Air raids were getting numerous. Almost all were at night. Many times about 2:00 A.M., we sat on our little benches in the back-yard shelter for hours and told stories or listened to the radio. "When it starts shaking," my brother said, "drop your damned knitting needles, or they'll fly right in your face." Well, I could keep on knitting most of the time; other parts of the city were hit hard. One night, the entire square of the Gestapo headquarters at Briennerstrasse was crumbled into a pile of rubble.

After hearing the news on the radio, we hopped on our bicycles and looked at the damage. I remember several people with big smiles on their faces who said: "What a perfect hit! *Volltreffer!*" But there were other hits that didn't seem as sensible and early on many mornings we worked in shifts to try and get to basement doors with signs of life behind them. I could never stay to see the people carried out or stumbling into the early morning light. I was always home much before my brother and his friends made it back. I sat in my room, sobbing for hours.

19. Lora

On one such morning, after the northern part of the city had completely burned down, my brother came home with a large birdcage fastened to his bike; in the bottom corner squatted a huge parrot, her tail burned off and her feathers singed. For days she sat there shivering all over until finally, she would take a couple of sunflower seeds, open her tremendous beak and say very clearly *"Guuuuuutes Lorchen!"*

We did find out that she belonged to an elderly couple and that they were not going to return to the city; they had lost their apartment that night and while they were in the basement shelter, the janitor had taken their dog and the parrot out of the burning building and had left the cage sitting in the street, where my brother found it. The couple, a writer and his wife, rented a room in a mountain village and took their dog with them, but they were glad to leave the bird with us for the time being, until they would have larger quarters again some day. It was years later that they came to take Lorchen back. Through the last of the war and several years after that, Lora was part of our household, and she was well worth her sunflower seeds, if I may say so.

When she had recuperated from the shock, she began to display a considerable vocabulary. She pronounced her words very clearly and loudly, so that every word of hers could be mistaken for a human voice. On warm days, we put her cage in the open window, where she fluttered her newly grown feathers in the sunlight and shouted loudly at every passer-by down the sidewalk: *"Haben Sie schon dafür bezahlt?"* (Have you paid for this yet?)

People would turn around to see who was bothering them and stand there laughing when they saw the parrot. Unfortunately, from our point of view, she also said "Heil Hitler." We tried to rid her of this habit, but she was a very old bird, and even though she learned new words with ease, she never forgot any of those that she knew. After she had been with us a while, she imitated perfectly Frau Fruhlich's peculiar way of laughing, she whistled for the neighbor's dog and called his name exactly as she had heard it, so that the dog would come rushing up the garden steps and wag its tail at her cage.

She was in this cage by the front entrance door most of the time, but could be let out on occasion, when everyone would be very careful not to get bitten: She had a big enough beak to take someone's finger half off, and we had to treat her with some respect. On the other hand, she was so much fun that we never considered giving her away; she said *"Guten Morgen"* cheerfully every day and she whispered *"Gute Nacht"* the last thing in the evening. She could sing and whistle and giggle, and generally imitate the tone of any conversation that was going on around her; there is no better cure for a beginning argument than this bird, imitating loudly the exact raised tone of voice that precedes a family squabble.

Also, at any sign of haste around her, she would wiggle back and forth on her perch and shout excitedly *"Schnell, schnell, eins-zwei-drei!"* (Hurry, hurry, one-two-three.) Undoubtedly, she had some notion about when to say what, and many a foreign visitor was shaken by the amount of German vocabulary this creature knew, compared with their own fluency with the language.

She also impressed the Gestapo one day. Their trips to

our house were getting more frequent. I remember one time, when several men in high boots and black uniforms were standing squarely in front of our door and demanded that we follow them. Into the long silence (our mouths usually dried up to the point where we could not pronounce a word) fell a triumphant bird call and the voice said unmistakably; *"Heil Hitler, haben sie schon dafür bezahlt?"* "Heil Hitler, have you paid for this yet?" The leader with the gun on his hip turned around and stuck his hand in the bird cage; "Who taught this bird to say 'Heil Hitler'?" he asked, and after her mighty wings stopped flapping and her claws had let go of the man's hand, he stumbled and fell on the wood box and we thought he was going to faint.

I bandaged his hand and gave him two aspirins for the pain, and we suggested that he go and have a doctor give him a shot against infection immediately. Without saying a further word, they all left silently. Before we crawled into our beds, we said *"Gute Nacht, liebes Lorchen."* And there she sat, on her perch, one foot tucked under her feathers for the night's rest, looking at us gravely from over her turned-up eyelids, and whispered; *"Ja, das ist ein guuuuuutes Lorchen."*

From then on, we tried to be more careful. We worked out a plan by which my mother, at the first sign of a bus parking by our house, would run down to the basement, slip though an opening in the brick garden wall, and under the bushes, enter Luschuwa's house unseen by anyone watching even the backyard.

As we had hoped, the simplest answer was that my mother wasn't available. This worked several times. But I got into the habit of watching the street at night for hours, and every car that drove by in the moonlight, made my heart go fast: What if it stops by our house? Once, the shadow of a man was visible crouched by the hedge half the night and I found out the next day that the girl from across the street had eloped with her boyfriend. I had stood by the window and watched him, I don't know how many hours. What a life!

20.　　Bombs

One summer night in July brought the worst attack on the city. It was rough right from the start, because my mother had misplaced the key to our self-dug shelter in the back yard. Our neighbors were already standing in front of the heavy cement door, the parrot was shouting at the top of her voice *"Schnell, schnell, schnell!"* (Fast) and Mother could not find her glasses and therefore no key; I was racing through her desk drawers, when the detonations started outside.

We both had to give up the search and were running through the yard, with all hell breaking loose around us; it was like the Fourth-of-July fireworks with flying objects thrown in for added excitement; we hung on to the padlock at the shelter door and started pulling; every crash gave us renewed strength and we pulled the entire cement lock right out of the door, with the padlock still intact. Where we took such strength from, I'll never know: but we all got down there without anyone hurt. So we sat there for the usual two hours, only this time, I wasn't knitting; the whole thing was shaking so badly, I was afraid that I would poke somebody with my knitting needles.

Undoubtedly, bombs had fallen nearby and any second we could get a direct hit. Luschuwa started to pray. I remembered that my brother once said that if we hadn't done our praying before that, it would be way too late now. The only time I really lost my nerve was when she started singing: "A Mighty Fortress Is Our God." She couldn't sing very well either. "It's a mighty shelter, Luschuwa, and the damn

101

thing is gonna hold up, see!" I tried to cheer her up, and we laughed a bit nervously.

When we emerged from our underground place of safety, the sky was light red all around. We sat in the basement for a while and had something hot, supposedly coffee. Then we went around the neighborhood to find what could be done. For hours we dug with pick-ax and shovel, because we could hear a persistent tap-tap-tap behind a pile of rubble.

Finally, some people stumbled out through a hole we made in the brick wall, and their faces were a ghostly white in the early dawn of the morning. Exhausted, we staggered home and saw my mother sitting on the front steps, reading the paper by the light of a burning city. Some paper boy had still made the rounds, for some blasted reason; but the news wasn't news any more, it had been printed before the air-attack.

After a short rest, we went out again; for a day or so, we tried to help the small troops of authorized people who were digging down into the basements of several collapsed apartment houses in the neighborhood. On the open field behind our house, they were lining up corpses for identification, big ones and small ones in a row, some very small indeed; those identified were removed for burial; the rest began to smell because it was July.

In the heat of the summer night, the smell kept us awake, and when I couldn't stand it any longer, I went out with some old sheets and rags and blankets and covered up the dead. Only when I had used sheets and blanket from my own bed could I fall on it and cry myself to sleep. What people were talking about was like a nightmare. Seventy percent of the city had been destroyed; there were reports of hundreds of people jumping into the Nymphenburg Canal burning like live torches; we sat around afraid of the next news to reach us; and then, all of a sudden everything changed: they had discovered a dud on the open field behind the house. This happened about two weeks after the night of the attack, and we were not really afraid that this bomb would still go off after this long a time, unless it was a time-bomb.

Pretty soon, they were evacuating the entire neighborhood. People were placed by the city officials in various hotels until the bomb would be detonated artificially. We had no identification that would allow us to check into a hotel like everyone else. My mother remained very calm: she said that we should refuse to evacuate; she figured that they would not insist, if we stayed casual about the whole thing.

Clear around one city block, checkpoints were set up to control everyone coming in and going out of our street. The three of us agreed that we would talk to all the guards and simply tell them that we were no more afraid of the old dud than they were. "As long as you are standing here to guard our safety, we are staying also and keep you company through the whole silly formality," we told them, and that worked. They were very nice about it.

Every time we had to go to a store for food, we had to pass the checkpoint; every few hours the guards changed: every time we talked to them, they laughed, because we told them that the stupid thing is not going to blow up now, after three weeks and that it wasn't worth the bother to move. Actually, we were much more afraid of the Gestapo than of the old bomb, to be sure.

One time, my mother came home with a pitcher of milk hanging from the handle bar of her bike: I saw her get off her bike and then I heard this command: "One, two, three, four," shouted by a sergeant's shattering voice. Mother dropped the milk can on the spot, came flying into the house, and down the basement steps. I came tumbling after her and threw myself down on the basement floor beside her, as we had been told to do by the guards. Then came a group of soldiers marching by and singing *"Auf der Heide blüht ein kleines Blümelein, und das heisst Erika"* (two-three-four). The replacement guards were marching up to the check point, and the sergeant was counting the bars for them to start their morale-boosting song! We were rolling on the basement floor, laughing; none of us were crying over the spilled milk!

Many times more, we had to take cover in the basement, alerted by the guards, who seemed most concerned for our safety; until one came over one day and told us that the thing was definitely going to be detonated by a command of soldiers who were specialists at such tasks. There we were, all lined up on the basement floor, with pillows over our heads and cotton in our ears in case the dud would explode during the transaction. At the appointed minute, something made a medium-loud "ffffffffffffft"-noise outside, and that was supposedly it. After all that trouble, the thing simply did "ffffffffffft," and was rendered harmless. We went out to look at the small round hole in the ground, left in the field next to our house by a bomb that didn't go off, and we felt very fortunate indeed. After that, all the people around the block moved back in and everyone assumed that we had come back first. It was no problem at all, and we were glad.

21.   Drugs

Our place of relative safety was difficult to heat, as we found out during the second winter of the war. As much as we had enjoyed the house and the open fields behind it in the summertime, in November came masses of snow blowing across the open space. The central heater, a large iron-cast stove in the basement, was efficient enough, but we did not have a lot of wood and coal to put into it. Our chances for obtaining a reasonable amount of fuel were not good, because food, medicine, fuel and other necessities had been rationed at the beginning of the war, and my mother was not eligible for any ration cards. It was obvious that this exclusion from the rationing system was capable of starving us, in case we didn't freeze.

We had only one answer for this desperate problem: the old saying that God is nearest where the need for Him is the greatest. As our need increased, we planned trips for finding help in the neighborhood. There were small stores and restaurants in the vicinity, whose owners turned out to be angels of mercy. Even though we didn't dare tell them the reason for our continuing state of emergency, they must have sensed the severity of our plight; without questions they shared with us for several years the meager supplies they were able to find for themselves. What the milkman, the grocery lady, the drugstore owner, the restaurant cook, and the family with the wood and coal supplies did for us during winter after winter of the war is too much to describe here.

With the last bit of wood and remains of packing boxes burning rapidly in the basement stove, we gathered around the second-floor outlet one evening. This was the only spot in the house where some warmth still was forthcoming. My mother promised that the very next morning, she would direct her efforts toward the fenced-off lot of the local coal shop, which was located on the other side of the open field. It was not far from us. She was successful and every week after, she came home from her begging trip with a bundle of firewood, a box full of burnable dust or a little sack full of coal.

The family with their *"Kohlenhandlung"* on the other side of the field gave us, week after week, during four successive winters whatever they could do without themselves; sometimes it was little, sometimes it was more, but without a doubt, it kept us from serious illness. The mere possibility of sickness was a terrible thought to face, since no welfare agency could do anything at all for us and no hospital could take us in. We had our doctor, who gave us the most excellent care and all medicines, but the rest of the tremendous load of our existence was carried by the local merchants.

One day, Mother returned from her weekly trip to the *"Kohlenhandlung"* with a young man trailing behind her. He was carrying two large sacks of coal. He was covered with black dust and did look as if he were going to disappear any minute under those enormous sacks.

After putting down the load, he exchanged a few words with us in French, hesitantly and sparingly, ate a snack that we put before him, and left. The coal man had asked my mother that day if she spoke French, and since she does, he suggested that she talk to a young workman, who was new in Germany and a native of southern France. The coal man thought that someone ought to talk to the young man in his own language, because he feared that there might be some-

106

thing wrong with him. "This fellow's melancholy eyes are beginning to bother me," he told my mother, "but I can't even talk to him and I don't know anybody else who could." This is how we found Robert and all our family feelings went out to him.

Robert became a daily visitor at our house, and he soon told us that he had run away from his home in Grenoble. He had entered Germany as a "Foreign Volunteer Worker," hoping to find here the youth organizations he believed in and for which Hitler's Germany was well known abroad. He said that he would never return home because of a terrible fight with his father, about political issues; he showed us pictures of a nice, middle-class house with Robert's parents and little sister on the front steps; there were pictures of Robert in the family car, portraits of Robert with his sister Mignon, a sweet-looking child with long curly hair; both were well dressed and well photographed. The three of us concluded at once that Robert's family background was as authentic as could be and ever so much better for him than what he could possibly find in Germany.

We resolved that all three of us were going to try to persuade Robert to return to his folks. We encouraged him to leave the labor camp for foreign workers and make his home with us, at least on an unofficial basis. He moved into my brother Gert's room, unpacked a big, old, heavy leather suitcase and became part of our family for six weeks.

At first, it was hard to believe what Robert told us about his political convictions and hopes. Obviously, he didn't know very much about Hitler's Germany; but he made fast progress in the language, displayed a dignified set of manners, worked very hard and smoked incessantly. He wore a large religious medal on a heavy chain around his neck, a fine piece of jewelry that I admired when he often left it lying on our bathroom shelf over the wash basin; this was strangely inconsistent for the National Socialist, which Robert proclaimed to be: wearing a religious medal! We kidded him about it and he was amiable and humorous in his replies.

"You're right about that," he would jokingly admit, "the Holy Virgin might soon be an outlaw in Germany since she was probably Jewish!" Ouch, yes, this was a bit inconsistent, but we decided that Robert was not really fear-inspiring, just a very young lad, inexperienced and often homesick, but rather nice. The only time he became disagreeable, was when we asked him what he was smoking constantly. His cigarettes looked different from any we had ever seen, as if they were home-made ones, but Robert assured us that he did not roll them himself, that someone was sending them to him from France.

"They are French cigarettes, that's what they are," he said. My mother said that French tobacco really was different, much stronger and darker than ours, but she asked Gert not to join in that habit because Robert smoked unbearable quantities. Even my brother, who got along with him very well otherwise, complained that Robert was driving him crazy by smoking all day and almost all night. What a habit like that must cost!

As the weeks went by and we became better acquainted, there were other things that we didn't like. As a matter of fact, we became increasingly fearful that Robert might belong to some kind of gang. One day, we met him downtown in the company of very rough-mannered guys. And when my mother told him that she didn't approve of the company he chose, Robert got very angry; he told her that he was over eighteen and intended to run around with his own friends and do what he pleased.

Mother got most upset about this, and she asked him to part company at once, either with his "friends," or with us.

108

It was amazing to us, after the good times we had since he joined us, that he did not hesitate a minute. As soon as we confronted him with this choice, which we had to do on account of our own vulnerability, he said that he did not wish to be treated like an underage child, that he got away from one family and was ready to part with any kind of parental supervision. He moved out immediately without leaving an address or sending a word of thanks.

We were rather relieved to have parted with him at this point. To think of the trouble he, as a National Socialist, could have started for us, not to mention his friends, who made all the difference in the world to us because we could not ever ask for any kind of police protection. What if they were criminals? No, we were not at all unhappy to be rid of him at that point. Actually, we were just lucky that he never returned with any of his buddies to give us a thing or two to remember. He himself was not that kind of person, to be sure, but his friends had us scared. We had the feeling that he enjoyed our hospitality enough not to want to hurt us in any way, but that he was too mixed up with that gang to be trusted any further.

After he had left, we did weigh the possibility once that he might have been on some kind of dope occasionally; some of his cigarettes smelled like it. I remember that we discussed the consequences of alerting authorities to what he might be getting into next. Later, just a little later, how we wished that we had done just that. If we had simply turned him in on the suspicion that he was using dope, he would have been sent back to his family, or at least to his country on a juvenile delinquency charge; compared to what happened to him in Munich, this would have been a truly great thing.

Since we were in hiding ourselves, we decided that by contacting anybody on account of Robert, we had a lot more to risk than he did. It was much too dangerous for us to deal with authorities of the "Reich," especially since he could have done us in, as a "National Socialist Sympathizer," to say the least. What if a charge of narcotics and such could not be substantiated? We were not that sure that dope was at the heart of this matter.

What we could possibly have done is to have written to his family. Again, they could only have gotten their son back home if they took our letter as a basis for authorities. Also, Robert had never once received a letter from them, nor had he written one that we knew of. We didn't have an address, and Grenoble is a good-sized city. As time went by and Robert stayed away, we assumed that the young man would mature in time. We were glad to forget the whole thing and very grateful that nothing really serious had developed from the episode.

What we did not know was that Robert and his "friends" were going to give us something to remember after all; that a very serious situation was going to develop into an absolutely horrifying conclusion. It was not until many months later, maybe even a year or so later, that the next and the last chapter of this episode was written.

It was written on the front page of the evening paper. I saw there, while bringing the paper in the house, a photograph of Robert's religious medal clear across the front page, the exact thing that had been on our bathroom shelf, Holy Virgin and on the chain. "Murder in Perlacher Park," the caption read beneath it. The purpose of the photograph was to publish the only existing identification for a corpse uncovered in the forest near our city. For a week, the details of a murderous story were in all the papers, but again, we could not contact authorities on account of our own situation.

It was very clear to us right then, that Robert was the

victim. The end result of the investigations did confirm his identity about a week later; and the story we followed in the papers during that week made very clear to us some of the aspects of our relationship with Robert, not only did we now understand the very frightening aspects that his presence held for us just before he left, but also the pleasant and the friendly aspects that we felt so strongly during his stay with us. All at once, we knew why we had to let him go so suddenly, but we were so justified in our trust in him and our sympathy for him. Yes, it was all so very understandable, now that it was too late.

Robert had been a member of a gang of young dope addicts, who had done many a "job," mostly petty thefts, in order to pay for the high cost of their habit. As several of them became bolder by repeated experience and more aggressive by necessity, they planned a regular robbery and Robert objected. He wanted to keep the gang on what he considered harmless levels. And in order to do just that, he went to the police and told them about his fear of a planned robbery that could easily result in homicide. The elderly gas station attendant whose life Robert feared for, got protection on account of the young man's report, but Robert himself did not.

Robert, apparently, had no idea what kind of people he was dealing with in this gang of his. Robert was simply making sure that his buddies' activities would stay within the bounds of what is known as youthful adventure. If they went any further than what he considered necessary, he would see to it that they got stopped. He told police that there was no need for concern as long as he was with them. He, Robert, could guarantee that these guys would not go too far. How far these guys were capable of going became evident after his gang had gone to Robert and nobody in town could identify his remains.

22.   Adolf Eichmann

Not a week went by without a major crisis. Every six months, there was the deportation order. We knew this document all too well by now; but this time there was an alarming difference: We were given only four days before departure. Four days would not be enough to take our necks out of the noose. Since the last "correspondence," we had heard much more about the sinister destination of such torturous journeys.

The reaction to this latest threat was sheer panic. We were up all night, we couldn't sleep. We ruled out going into hiding, because we would have to split up; the people who would be courageous enough to hide us would be put in mortal danger by our presence; most of all, should one of us be caught, it would mean torture to give away the hiding place of the other two. They had ways to make people talk. Leaving the country would take much more time.

In the morning, only three days left, I was given a tranquilizer; when I came to, Mother and Gert had decided that Frank Becker was the only person with the means to interfere on such short notice. Several desperate phone calls resulted in a plan. Gert was to take the night train to Berlin, where Frank had a connection to the Reichs-Sicherheits-Hauptamt, Security Headquarters of the Reich. He was to call at Prinz Albrechtstrasse at two o'clock sharp the next day. Frank was optimistic; he said he had arranged for an appointment with Karl Adolf Eichmann.

Eichmann was jokingly called the "King of Jews," because he was in charge of all Jewish problems. Frank said this was the only person who could phone the Munich Gestapo at the last minute to put a stop to the deportation, theoretically. Mother had a complete breakdown; she lay lifeless on her bed in the living room and looked like a corpse already. Gert told me to call him at Kempinski's restaurant at four o'clock the next day to find out how things were going. When he left I was absolutely certain that his news would be the worst ever; most of all I feared that Gert would be arrested at this "illustrious" location. I had told him about that when he left. "Nonsense," was his answer, "I was in combat on the Russian front, remember. He wouldn't dare to do that." I took the phone number and promised to call, there wasn't anything else I could do. Or was there?

I was not able to sleep and conjured up a back-up plan, in case Gert was turned down. A friend had brought us a couple of chickens to supplement our meager diet. We kept them in the basement for the daily eggs they produced. If everything else failed, I resolved to whack the chicken's heads off, gather their blood in a bowl, and pour it into Mother's bed, claiming that she could not be taken. The next day went by somehow.

At four, I dialed the number with shaking hands. For the first time, Gert sounded beaten; "All is lost, we are finished." Eichmann had listened patiently to the soldier's story, to his plea for mercy. Eichmann did not reply and Gert was encouraged to mention our father's death at age forty-four. Isn't it a terrible mistake to treat his family so brutally? Gert continued as long as the ascetic-looking man would listen. Suddenly, Eichmann got up behind his desk and shouted: "Get out of here at once, you miserable creature! To appear in my office, that is the audacious impudence of a Jew! To take the place of a pure German," his voice got louder and louder. "Get out!"

113

This is what my brother told me on the phone. He was crying. My thoughts were going around in circles: "Gert won't be here when they come tomorrow morning! Mother and I will be alone. What an awful, uneven situation that will be! I will have to play the last card I have left: Mother will lie in a bloodbath and the Gestapo will be repulsed, they won't want to touch her." All night, I prepared for the most dangerous day of my short life. I prayed to Almighty God.

In the morning I was very calm; I felt numb, as if one could only be afraid so long. "The devil loses or the devil wins and life would not be desirable in that case." I managed to kill only one chicken and then, my stomach turned over, I had enough blood in my bowl. I took it to my mother's bed, where she seemed almost lifeless. When I heard a bus driving up, I poured the blood all over Mother's bed and ran to the window.

In the early morning light, I saw a dozen or so men jumping from the bus and heading for our door. Too many men to pick up one sick little woman, too many SS to keep the door locked.

The leader, a Sturmführer of the SS, pushed me aside when I opened. "Where is Sara Leonie?" he demanded, and the other men swarmed all over the house, two went upstairs, one in the kitchen, two in the basement, one in the bathroom, two on the balcony. "*Sturmführer*," I shouted, "she is much too sick to be taken from her bed, she has suffered a hemorrhage!"

"That's what they all say, where is she?" He burst into the living room and in front of Mother's bed. "Get up and give me your envelope with your papers! Where is your baggage?" "I told you she can't get up, the doctor said she might die." "Ridiculous, don't play games here, get her up!" I took the blanket off and she lay there in a bloodbath.

114

The leader stopped hollering and I used this advantage. "I need your name, *Sturmführer*," I explained quietly, "because my brother is at the Ministry of Propaganda for a conference with Dr. Goebbels." I was so confused that I got Eichmann mixed up with Joseph Goebbels. "My brother is a front soldier and came to Berlin to confer with the Minister on behalf of his mother." "My name is Lindner and I have orders." He was less sure of himself. "Orders are orders, don't waste my time!"

I didn't let go. "You'll see, your orders will be revoked, you are right, it will be a waste of your time." He was not convinced. "How do I know that this is true? You could tell me anything, most of them do!"

"Would you be good enough to exchange phone numbers with me? My brother is going to call this afternoon, and I will tell him that you need the word of Dr. Goebbels himself. If you wish to talk to my brother, here is the number in Berlin." I handed him the phone number of the Kempinski restaurant. *If he calls the number right now, he can shoot me.*

He actually pointed his pistol at me. "If you are trying to trick me, you will be sorry! If we don't have word from Dr. Goebbels's office, we will be back tomorrow at the same time. We need confirmation of your story by five o'clock this afternoon. I'll be in my office until five. After that, it will be too late and you will get to know me better tomorrow morning."

To give him this phone number was a kind of madness. Whatever got into me to do such a thing? Before my unbelieving eyes, he called his SS men and they left. They actually left. It seemed like a miracle. There was no time for contemplation.

When Gert called to find out what happened, I didn't make much sense. We both felt that there was no more hope. Gert wanted to take the night train home, so that he would be there when "they" returned. I did not believe he could be back early enough. There was a long silence, then he said he could fake a phone call from the Ministry of Propaganda. "Try that," I agreed, "leave a message for Lindner." "I don't think I can make it believable," his voice sounded as if he was crying. "Goebbels speaks with a Rhineland dialect that is too difficult to fake; also, he doesn't have a thing to do with deportations, but he could call off an order just the same."

My brain replayed the awful scene of the morning. "Gert, the SS man said that he would have to get word from Dr. Goebbels's office by seventeen o'clock today, from his OFFICE."

"My God, it's a quarter past four! I can hear the minutes ticking away. Give me the number of Lindner's office, and I'll do it right now." He sounded so disheartened I hung up the phone crying hopelessly. On the way back to his hotel, Gert was thinking feverishly about the details. The following is an exact translation of his own account, written in German,

My thoughts were racing. Even if I impersonate Reichsführer Jung, the Munich Gestapo could resort to ringing the Ministry back to ask another question and the hoax would bust right there. I will have to play it so they can't call back. Surely members of the Gestapo are like other government employees, putting down their pens on the stroke of five. Minutes later, there would be a nightshift answering the phone.

Ten minutes before five, I went to the hotel switchboard. "I need an immediate connection with a number in Munich." I handed the operator the number and a fifty-Mark bill. "Please listen to me and do me this favor: The number is that of a government office and under no circumstance are they to find out that the call is from a hotel desk. All you have to say is, 'One moment, please, I connect.' It is

116

very important, please do this for me." I looked at her imploringly and she nodded her head silently.

I went into the booth and waited. I looked at my watch, a few more minutes and the phone should ring. It rang. I dried off my sweating hands and lifted the receiver with shaking fingers. "Gestapo Munich, telephone exchange." With the deepest voice I could manage, I said, "Give me extension three-five-nine." "Extension doesn't answer at this time, probably closing time." I had a good feeling. That's what I was hoping for. The first hurdle is taken! This gave me enormous courage and I spoke louder and sharper. "Listen, this is the Ministry of Propaganda in Berlin, Office of Dr. Goebbels. Your name?"

"Scharführer Rittler," answered the man, a little intimidated. "Okay, Scharführer, listen to me carefully. On order of Dr. Joseph Goebbels, we have to get a message to Sturmführer Lindner, extension three-five-nine. You are to give it to him first thing tomorrow morning when he comes in. The doctor reserves the right of decision for himself on behalf of the Jewish widow Sara Leonie Gundersheimer, residing Hofenfelsstrasse #54. Scharführer, are you writing this down?" "*Jawohl*, I'm writing!"

"The final decision is solely reserved for the Minister, you understand? It means that the deportation scheduled for tomorrow morning is revoked. Repeat what you wrote down."

"What was your name again?"

"Listen to me, Rittler; you are personally responsible that Sturmführer Lindner gets this message when he opens his office in the morning. Do you understand?" "*Jawohl!*"

Just when I was ready to put down the receiver, Rittler asked the fateful question: "Your name and number?" My heart stood still. Anything but this question. All had gone so well. Now, I'll have to throw all my authority on the scale. I shouted: "Man, didn't you hear me? This is Reichsleiter Jung, Office of Propaganda; you should know where to find me!"

Here ends the translation of Gert's writing that he put on paper on the overnight train from Berlin. Both of us spent a dreadful night, because the outcome of our desperate maneuver was more than doubtful. If Lindner gets his message this morning, he might call the number I gave him, gets Kempinski's restaurant and return with a righteous fury; if Rittler had second thoughts after Gert's call, and recommends a confirming connection with Dr. Goebbels's office, all three of us would be beaten, disposed of, shot. Why wouldn't anybody call Eichmann, who is in charge of deportations? Eichmann would immediately make the connection with his visitor from the day before.

The return of the Gestapo this morning means that all three of us are out of luck. It is so obvious that both Gert and I are behind this grotesque swindle, the basement of the Brienner-Turken Strasse, the Gestapo cellar, is where we will end up for certain. I had faced death before, but torture was something else! Exhaustion was taking over, my nerves were giving out.

Just before 9:00 A.M., Gert walked in the front door: "Have they been here? Where is Mother?" We both sat by Mother's bed for the next few hours. Every kind of noise sent something down our spines that felt like boiling oil. I must have run to the window dozens of times to see if the bus had arrived. The tension continued all day, after all, "they" had to make an extra trip, one that was not scheduled, and that could happen twenty-four hours a day.

As soon as the Gestapo finds out that they had been tricked, they would show up. How could they not know that they had been fooled? The whole fantastic story was so unbelievable; nobody would ever find it credible! Weeks went by and nothing happened. Slowly, we realized that the crisis was over, really, and that the next transport would not be organized until six months later.

23.   Well Meant Warnings

The six months between deportations had to be well used to prepare our next move. Friends tried to help, but nobody really knew what to do. Somebody told us to buy cyanide on the black market in case our luck would run out. Advice of that sort met with Mother's stern disapproval. "We are not going to do the job for them; if they come here to kill us, they'll have to do it themselves." I have since tried to forget these words, but I never could.

During the first winter of war on the Eastern front, we had received a telegram from a long-time friend of my father's, Uncle Fred. He had been drafted for the offensive in Poland. His telegram informed us that he was using a short leave to come and see us. I could tell by Mother's crestfallen face that nothing pleasant was to be expected from this visit.

When he arrived in full uniform, he first let us know the purpose of his effort. We had prepared dinner for him, but before we could start eating, he took a big revolver out of his briefcase and placed it on our dining table. He told us what he had seen in Poland with his own eyes. He had been inside one of the death camps and he had come here to warn us.

"If they ever come here to arrest you," he informed us, "do not under any circumstances, go with them! As a friend of the family, I would prefer that you shot yourselves before they can take you. I made the long trip to warn you," he concluded with tears in his eyes.

"Mein Gott!" said my mother and removed the plates from the table. "We are grateful for your love and appreciate

119

the very timely warning." We managed to say good-bye to him; when we had closed the door behind him, we looked at each other. My teeth were chattering. I had never seen a revolver this close. Mother picked up the gun with two fingers. Gert blinked his eyes at me and muttered, "You wait and see." She held the revolver in her hand with outstretched arm, as if to keep it far away from her, slowly she moved over to the window. "Open it! Let me get rid of this murder weapon before I get mad at anybody!" With an energetic jolt, she flung the gun out into the icy winter night. "Children," she said while closing the window, "we are not going to take the dirty business off their hands," and *That was that,* I thought, but not my brother:

"What do you mean?" He laughed. "That thing is worth more than a hundred marks! I can now try to dig it up again in five feet of snow and even if I find it, drying it off will take half the night. I will take it to a pawnshop in the morning and try to get some money for it." We went out into the backyard with a flashlight and found the frightful thing in the wintery mass of white powder. It was fun taking it apart and putting it back together, drying it, oiling it, not being afraid of it!

The next morning, Gert took off on his bike, the precious box clamped behind him on the wire rack. He came back with a sum that was considerably more than we had expected. "Uncle Fred has done a good deed! Perhaps not exactly in the way it was intended, but, as it turns out, I am so relieved to be able to pay off some of our debts."

24.   The Fruits of Madness

The first one to disappear was Mother's youngest cousin, Gisela; she went into hiding and at the time, I didn't know where she was; somebody said she went to Switzerland. Years later, she told me that a Swiss businessman took her into his mansion in Heidelberg. He had a certain amount of immunity from German government agencies, but he had demands and conditions. Knowing that the Gestapo always searched first and asked questions later, he determined that nobody could visit Gisela at his house, because nobody was to know that she was there. He took a certain amount of risk there and did this for years. Gisela survived the Nazis and was the only blood-relative we had left after the Second World War.

A colleague of Mother from the time she had worked in the film industry, solved his predicament by disappearing into the cleaning closet of the night train to Berlin. The conductor of the train was in on it, of course. When the train stopped in the middle of the night in some obscure little town, Erich was let out to take his nightly walk along the platform. I was there when somebody asked him after the war, how he could possibly have endured this for years (four, I believe). I thought his answer was remarkable: "I was extremely lucky! The train had a restaurant car and what my friend brought me was very good food; I scratched out a little peephole in the milk glass window, so that I could see the landscape go by; I counted cows, horses, sheep, even people, and I was never caught; considering the alternative of a death camp, I had no complaints." I found his account so amazing that I could never forget it.

Friends of ours, Frau Castello and her teenage daughter, gave us an example of the danger we were in at all times. She was a widow like my mother; her husband had lost his life in 1923. Sixteen National Socialists were shot down by the Munich police in front of the Feldherrnhalle (a monument from the First World War). After Hitler came to power in 1933, he placed an "eternal" honor guard by the sixteen stone coffins, which had the names of the sixteen Nazi heroes engraved on each coffin. Every year on the anniversary of the street battle in November, a most solemn celebration was held on the spot where the first sixteen Nazis had fallen dead: their names were called out through a loudspeaker and a voice answered "HERE" in their place. So it happened every year that the name Castello was brought to mind on the loudspeaker.

There was, however, a complication not to be overlooked: his wife was Jewish. At first, the Munich Gestapo didn't quite know what to do about that! Frau Castello told my mother that she felt safe in her unique situation; they wouldn't dare, she thought. She lasted until 1943, when the Gestapo arrested her with her daughter, who tried in vain to use her father's fame to save her mother. She was in Theresienstadt camp for only two years until 1945 and the end of the Nazi regime, but died shortly after she was liberated. That they deported her seemed to me the moment of truth for our own chances. Gert's uniform would not be enough to protect us either, so I thought. Mother would cut short any kind of discussion on such issues by saying: "They have definitely taken leave of their senses!"

It seems even in retrospect that the only answer to these madhouse tactics was to act even crazier than they did. Many times, we considered leaving the country; but every time my mother decided to stay; this meant outdoing our persecutors as our only chance for survival. The one factor in my mind that made our mother different from anyone I ever knew was her absolute optimism, her certainty that she would succeed.

Actually, there were many people sure that nobody would harm them in Germany, and who perished as a result. Even though I was too young to make such far-reaching decisions on my own, I sensed very clearly that Mother's optimism was not based on anything realistic. When we had offers to be taken across the border into Switzerland, she would go through the whole process of planning our departure and all of a sudden she would say, "I really would prefer that the three of us would die right here." And that was that. We had our pictures in a passport with a false name, we had people who would accompany us over the border, but we did not have Mother's consent.

What we did have were a few extremely courageous friends. They took many chances with their own lives to help us along. Several doctors, who must have been more committed to saving lives than some of their colleagues, went to Gestapo offices and declared separately that my mother's tumor was cancerous and that she should be left to die. They gave her three months to live. Since the next transport would leave in six months, it was apparently satisfactory to inquire at that time as to "the woman's certified and certain death." We knew perfectly well that this particular excuse would not work a second time. Would six months be long enough to devise a plan to prevent organized execution?

25. The Captain

Christine was my best friend from elementary school. She lived with her mother, and she was a very serious and fragile-looking girl. Perhaps it was my brother's constant kidding and teasing, perhaps we just had much in common, but Christine had been a part of my life since we were both ten years old. She seemed very shy to anyone who didn't know her well. Her long, ratty braids did not improve her appearance; she looked like a poor little orphan. When I got to know her better, I realized that Christine was an actress, not the glamorous, elegant kind, but one who would play Antigone or Iphigenia.

Her life seemed to me uneventful and protected, yet strangely pessimistic. This was in contrast to my family's unfounded optimism; in any case, we needed each other. Christine's mother remained distant; I was not able to find out much about her, except that she lived for her music. She gave singing lessons, and occasionally she would give a concert.

During the third winter of the war, the cultural life of the city had come to a standstill. Theaters and concert halls were still in existence, but there was no heating. Only the greatest music enthusiasts came to sit wrapped in their coats and the orchestras had great difficulty playing instruments in sub-freezing temperatures. As long as the city had not been bombed heavily, they performed.

Around holiday time in December, Christine's mother accepted an engagement to sing at the Royal Theater. It was to take place on a Wednesday night and the Saturday before that, Christine called me in desperation. Her mother, she said, had saved a few yards of brocade material and had given them to a dressmaker to sew a gown. Weeks before the concert, they had tried to contact the seamstress only to find out that she had something else to do. They had gotten their material back and were trying to start all over at this late date.

I was good at designing and making clothes. Doing alterations and sewing all kinds of garments meant that I got some groceries in exchange. The idea of working on a formal, a thing that was not much in demand at the time, was exciting to me. When Christine and her mother could stop by to have the measurements taken, it was Sunday afternoon. The concert was to be next Wednesday.

I had two and a half days to do the job. I promised my friends that the formal would be ready by Wednesday afternoon. I started immediately and spent all of Sunday night designing the gown. It was going to be something special! Monday morning, I started to cut the fabric, but when my friends came back in the evening for the first fitting, it was far from perfect. I rearranged things, spent all day Tuesday sewing. Late that day, Christine's mother came back again and we were delighted. I was so proud of myself; I did not even feel exhausted. I had to keep working all night; for fear that I might not finish on time. The full skirt out of tulle and the satin slip, plus the brocade overcoat had such endless hems that I was still sewing Wednesday afternoon.

We had agreed to meet at the concert hall to deliver the gown. I barely made it in time for the performance. I helped the star of the evening into my creation, and she handed me a complimentary ticket. Here I was in my old skirt and blouse; there was no time to comb my hair or wash my face. Slaphappy from lack of sleep, I did not care. I simply had to see that formal and what it looked like on the stage. My seat was in the first row and I noticed several ladies in mink coats. As the lights went down, there were still some seats being filled right and left of me. Christine's mother took her place by the concert grand and I could not believe my eyes: She was so very beautiful! Around her tall and bony figure were the yards and yards of tulle that spread into a pleasing circle. Over all that fell the coat of brocade, simple, sleeveless and collarless. Relieved and satisfied, I was just ready to close my eyes and listen to the familiar voice, when I had the notion that someone in the seat next to mine was staring at me.

No wonder, I thought, *I must look terribly out of place.* The glorious coloratura voice of my friend filled the hall, but that person next to me was not looking at the stage, but was watching me. *I am such a mess that somebody can't get over it.* I closed my eyes, but I took a glimpse sideways and looked into the eyes of a young man. I saw the Iron Cross with Gold Leaves at the front of a uniform. *Don't tell me I won't be able to hear the well-deserved rest of this concert! I will simply ignore him, just let him stare.*

As the audience started clapping after the first song, he said in a low voice: "That is the most wonderful dress I have ever seen!"

In a kind of intimate way, he whispered, "You are the designer, aren't you?" Immediately I was afraid that he might guess a few other things about me and I resolved to leave at the start of intermission.

Before intermission started, he blurted out his entire story: "I am on a few days furlough from the Russian front, and I have buried my mother this morning. Right in this concert hall full of happy people, I am going out of my mind! You are the only person here who might understand what is happening to me; you are different from the others! I

126

need you for just a little while, the short time I have here at home." He tried to hold my hand, but I got up and ran away.

As always when I was upset, I walked and walked, tears streaming down my face. *You certainly picked the wrong person, poor soldier.* I tried to regain my composure. At least he was not following me. *Poor soldier, not really!* I thought. With that Iron Cross on his chest, he must have done something special. Also, he had the epaulettes of a captain and was much too young for that. "Good riddance," I sighed. "Somebody else will have to console him. I do feel sorry for him, but this is just not for me!" By the time I reached the next streetcar stop, I felt better, got into the next car, and sat down in the back. I fell asleep immediately, remembering that the West Cemetery was the end of that line and that the conductor would wake me when we were there.

Somebody woke me all right, but it wasn't the conductor. "End of the line!" he said. I thought it sounded symbolic and I was frightened. "What are you doing here?" was all I could mumble. "I did find you," he said cheerfully, "the last wish of the doomed man is granted!" Those words fit right into my train of thought: *He knows what's waiting for him at the Russian front, and he is cracking up.*

We were standing at the station late at night, and there was nobody else around. He kept talking in a persuasive sort of way, telling me that his uncle lived a ten-minute walk away. "My mother left a note for me; I would like to show it to you tomorrow. We are Catholic and she writes that she left me in the special grace of the Virgin Mary. I believe the Madonna has sent to me! I am safe." Of course, I knew all about that! I forgot that I was afraid of him and realized that this officer with his shiny cross was in far greater danger than I was. I felt ashamed of my selfishness.

"I will read your mother's letter tomorrow," I finally said. He walked me home, and we sat on the front doorstep in the cold of the winter night. He spoke again of his mother, of his childhood, how much he loved her. "She always prayed for me and now, I need you to pray for me, or I will never come home again." He cried on my shoulder. I remembered that he had buried his mother that very morning; when everything happens so fast, it can get to be too much! I knew that all too well. How tragic was this war, what hell on earth.

I woke Mother as soon as I got in the house; she was not happy about my story. "We don't have enough trouble of our own," she said, "you have to bring me home some more in the middle of the night." After some thought, we decided that we were not going to tell him about our situation at that time, but to wait until he left two days later. Just before his departure, I would mention to him that his Holy Virgin was Jewish. He can then think about it and write to let us know what he intends to do about it, if anything. Maybe he'll forget the whole thing after our bit of new information. Who knows? We all had learned not to think too far ahead in times like these.

I got a few hours of sleep and at six in the morning, he rang the doorbell. Good God, why would anybody be in such a hurry? We fixed a little breakfast and Mother said in the kitchen: "You certainly picked a handsome guy!" I didn't answer, because I didn't pick him. Somewhere in the back of my tired mind flashed the thought that he'd be more beautiful in the grave. I did not admit that suspicion into my consciousness, because one cannot really be sure about it.

Hanni was chatty and amiable, and he asked Mother if I was engaged to someone or had a steady boyfriend. She said she hadn't quite gotten his name. He was Hans Hoelzel, Hanni for short, he said and his aunt and uncle were giving him a farewell party that evening. Would I be able to come over? Mother was immovable, she was sorry to refuse, but she had other plans for me that evening. He asked to use the phone and while he was busy, I told Mother that I didn't believe this uncle really existed; but he could not ask me over if aunt and uncle were purely an invention of his.

As it turned out, they were not only real, they came over fifteen minutes later; they lived a few blocks away in an apartment house next to the city's gas plant. He was a retired employee of the utility company and his wife said that Hanni was her nephew; they had known him all his life and they wanted to invite me personally. Mother was much friendlier and seemed to agree that I was to be the guest of honor at tonight's party. They still had business to settle about Hanni's mother, they excused themselves and left us in a state of excited confusion.

I got a few hours sleep and found time to wash my hair. I was looking foreword to being the guest of honor. I had never been the guest of honor before. I found a little present for the young man, a collection of poems that he could take with him as a souvenir; it was to be his last evening at home.

The party was much more festive than I expected with about ten guests, all friends of Hanni's. After dinner, Hanni had a present for me too; before I could open it, his uncle took me by the arm and led me into the next room. "If you have a heart, my dear, you accept him; he needs someone to write letters to, who will write to him, please don't say no." He must have feared that the "surprise" would be too overwhelming for me. I went to powder my nose, comb my hair, and decided I could answer his letters.

Hanni opened the present for me and put the ring on my finger. I embraced him with genuine feeling. I tried to avoid the thought that just twenty-four hours ago, I had not yet met this young hero. With a glass of wine, I washed down the feeling that this was a tragic event. Hanni seemed happy. He took me home at ten o'clock, kissed me by the door politely, and assured me that we would be married soon. "I will call my commander early in the morning; ask for a few more days furlough. You'll see, everything will turn out perfectly!" I was convinced that he would get his wish; since he seemed to know how to get everything else he wanted, I would tell him tomorrow about our "situation"; I was getting used to the speed that he brought with him.

Back in the house, my mother had objections. "You don't know him; you need to ask for the time to get to know him better." "Of course I will do that," I reassured her, "I will ask for more time." Finally, she said it was up to me.

Hanni was at the door at nine o'clock, with a bouquet of flowers. I didn't have the slightest idea what I would say. Didn't I sign a statement once about the German armed forces, etc.? Hanni was quite different from the day before, much more serious, and almost sad. He asked Mother to give us some time alone. Then he pulled me close to him, held me tight, and told me that the extra days he had asked for had not been granted. "I will have to leave within the hour," he said, "my driver is waiting outside. I'll have to catch the train east at eleven o'clock." There it is, the train again, another kind of train going east, not the train that could deport my mother, but a death train just the same.

A voice inside me would not be silenced: "Hanni, let this train go, go into hiding until the war is over, it won't take much longer." Why don't I tell him the whole truth right now, maybe he can take it? Then I said, "Didn't you tell me that you believe in the Madonna and that she will protect you? Do you realize that the Holy Family was actually Jewish?"

There was a long silence, and then he spoke with the determination that was characteristic for him. "No, that was way back in Palestine. In Germany, I mean here in Bavaria, she would not be Jewish. Why, do you have somebody Jewish in your family background?"

When he said that about Bavaria, I lost confidence; there could be consequences if he told his commander about me. "Why, do I look it?" He laughed, obviously relieved, but then he added, "It would not make any difference, because I have been nominated to receive the Knight's Cross. It is awarded to people who have reached their sufficiency; it is worn hanging from your collar, so you won't vomit. I should receive that within a few weeks and then I can marry anybody I please, nobody can put anything in my way. When I come back, we can start a nice little family, ah, when I come back!"

I had the feeling that he could succeed; he seemed to get anything he wanted, like my brother, or he could come back wounded, like my father, decorated and with the Knight's Cross. Who was I to be pessimistic, I didn't know the future. "I have to go now," he interrupted my thoughts; "will you be true to me?"

"And you," I answered mechanically, "will you remain true to me?" He did not answer; instead, he said, "It will be a long way back to the front lines. I will have so much time to think of you."

"I'll write to you every day, Hanni, when one day, you don't get a letter, you'll know it is on the way and will get there tomorrow." "Yes, my love, I believe that you will wait for me and that I will come back because you wait for me."

Hanni turned around and walked away, leaving the door open behind him. I wanted to call out "Don't go!" but he was walking down the steps, through the front garden, and got into the car that was waiting outside. He was gone. After Hanni's departure, letters were going and coming; he wrote twice a week at first, less and less as time went by. This could be understood and expected since bad news came from the Russian front. More and more, the news was interpreted as a "successful retreat."

Early in 1944, the Russian campaign took a turn for the worse and the absence of news from my fiancé was termed normal under the circumstances. I kept writing, mostly because I was pleased to consider myself a bride and I imagined marvelous things that Hanni would do for Mother and me, once he was back home. Maybe he would remain as lucky as he had been so far, maybe he would return wounded. When his letters ceased to arrive, I got in touch with his aunt and uncle, but they didn't know any more than I did. It was an uneasy wait; I read his letters over again and found them very poetic, but strangely impersonal. He had written about occasional weekend activities, sunsets over the Russian plains and his love for me; he never once mentioned our last conversation and he never asked how we were getting along. Mother mentioned that it could not be different, because he didn't know me. I was more inclined to believe that he had forgotten these two days in his turbulent life. None of my letters was ever returned, it was still possible that he was receiving them.

In February of 1944, a large envelope and a small package arrived in our mailbox. I was informed that Captain Hans Hoelzel had died in combat on December 26, 1943. In the package were some of his belongings, including the book I had given him, but no note to me personally. I did the best I could do by retreating into what I call a state of suspended animation. No thinking allowed! Several weeks after the bad news, I dreamed about him once. In his usual determined way, he told me "It's all right with me, my child, you needn't pray for me, it's not necessary."

When I woke up I had the feeling that he must be far away from me—because he called me "child."

Mother tried to help me: "He might have had several

short-lived engagements like the one he forced on you, don't make too much out of these two days with him." This was good advice and I tried to remove this painful episode from my memory.

Even though I managed to put my heart at rest, the clear insight into the life and death of just one of those "brave soldiers" left a cold emptiness that would not go away, ever. My brother found out later that the Knight's Cross, that basis for Hans Hoelzel's hope for our future, was awarded to him "posthumously," on February 23, 1944 (see Document section).

26.   My Brother the Spy

Many stories were told among friends that hinted at ridding Germany of Adolf Hitler. One such story was about a farmer's son, who went swimming in the river, when he saw a man drowning in the middle of the stream; the young man risked his life and saved the stranger, who thanked the young man for the rescue.

"I will grant any wish you might have, no matter how costly," promised the stranger. "You have saved the life of your Führer, Adolf Hitler." There was a long silence and then the lad said: "Let me have a state funeral with military honors." "A funeral, that is remarkable! Why do you want a funeral?" exclaimed Hitler. "Well," said the youngster, "when my father finds out that I saved your life, he is going to kill me."

There were people who did more than tell funny stories: a resistance movement, mostly students at the University of Munich. Gert told me that they printed leaflets and distributed them all over southern Germany. I never saw any of the leaflets, but feared that they didn't know their own government very well. Anyone who suggested that Germany would surely lose the war and that we would save lives by surrendering right now would be executed for treason.

Five students and their professor, Kurt Huber, were arrested on February 18, 1943. They were known as the organization of "The White Rose." The fate of the brother and sister team was publicized as an example for those who dared to fool the Gestapo. They let it be known that the Munich Gestapo had a guillotine in the basement of Briennerstrasse headquarters. Everybody thought that the guillotine had gone out of style after the French Revolution? Could this happen in the twentieth century? We got the answer on February 22, 1943. For my brother and me, it hit closer to home than we dared to admit to ourselves, or to each other.

There also lies the answer to the question "Why didn't anybody devise an assassination plot?" Finally, on July 20th 1944, ten months before the dissolution of the Third Reich, army brass set a bomb under the table where Hitler was seated. Seconds before it was set to go off, Hitler went over to point out something on a map. The plot failed and all participants were hanged, not shot, but hanged.

All these different ways of killing spread paralysis among otherwise courageous people. Many were not afraid to die, but torture was feared by all. Civilized people were not able to deal adequately with this aspect of the Nazi regime. Decades later, the mention of the six victims of the "White Rose," five of them in their early twenties, elicits a squirm and a kind of disbelief. Considering the flyers of the "White Rose," filled with humanitarian concerns, history, philosophy and poetry, set against the brutality of the National Socialists, what could one expect? The outcome was more devastating than expected: Christoph Probst, father of three, and the two Scholls, Hans and Sophie, were dead four days after their arrest, decapitated. The so-called people's court was in a hurry to avoid publicity.

When Willy Graf, Alexander Schmorrell and Professor Kurt Huber were executed later that year, nothing leaked to the news media. The German Department of Justice did not even retract their verdict of treason until 1980, when a movie called *White Rose* brought up the onerous event.

My brother had insisted, from the very beginning, that the only way to beat this murderous gang was by their own methods, namely by inspiring fear. His theory led him all the way to the "*Abwehr*," the German counter-espionage service, where he did nothing but inhibit the Gestapo from getting on our case.

There was always a six-month space between transports. We could use this time to prepare our next move; there would be another attack, to be sure. Gert made another application to the army command in Berlin; their reply was negative (see copy of the original document in the Document section). They respected his dedication and his courage, but "a return to active service in the armed forces is not possible because of the existing laws."

Gert was extremely depressed and contemplated our situation continuously. I tried to comfort him: "If you had died on the battlefield, we would be without protection just the same. Don't you prefer the way it is?"

"Dying for the homeland is a rather thankless task, and I am very glad to be out of that one; but I have to think of the next transport and I don't know what I can do about it now."

Gert never stopped trying to find the way out of the dilemma. His newest plan was kept a secret, and I was not informed. All I knew was that he had run into Georg Neuner in a coffee shop and that the two of them were hatching a new scheme. I found the silence nerve-wracking. Then, when I least expected it, Gert blurted out: "The world of espionage is weird and fascinating. I am going to be a spy." I wanted to know more: "What are you going to do and who are you going to spy for?"

"Well," he said, "it's like this: If Hitler's war keeps on going, I will spy for Germany. If we lose the war in the near future, I am a German Jew, spying for the English; it doesn't

136

matter because the real reason is our mother and you, my beloved sister!"

Georg had introduced him to his Secret Service superior, Herr Dauser, and they designed a plot straight out of "The Life of Riley." It was so involved. I didn't understand most of it. All I got was a few glimpses of the main issues: Gert was honest about his intent to save his family and the S.D. boss bought it (The S.D. was the German equivalent of the CIC). Georg Neuner had convinced the liaison agents Ganzer and Kurz that Gert could be sent to Spain to obtain a false passport for his mother. Once there he could contact the British secret service to help him in his desperate attempt to get his family out of Germany; they could check the facts of his dilemma and would find the urgency believable. In return for a visa for Spain, Gert would bring back all that he would find out about the British connection.

I was pessimistic: "O God, what have you wrought!" I was sure all of it was extremely dangerous! When Gert left for Madrid, I warned him: "I bet you don't even have your toothbrush with you." He did not have his toothbrush. He went upstairs to the bathroom and came back with his toothbrush in his breast pocket. "I'll be back when my mission is accomplished," he said and he was off to the airport.

Two weeks later, he was back. All he said about it was, "Mission accomplished," it left a lot to the imagination. I kept asking him. Much later, he described the adventure: He had made connection with the British and he asked them for help. A Dr. van Acker, a physician, applied for a Swiss passport in London and accepted Gert's offer to work for the British (in Germany). While waiting for the passport for Mother, Gert had a sleepless night and decided not to work as a British spy. "As soon as they give me a number, I will be a double agent;" he concluded and called the airport for the next flight home. "In Munich," he finished, "I can tell them whatever, I made connection and the rest is my business. A spy never gives away all his information, anyway." I don't know what Gert told them in Munich; they knew Dr. van Acker as a British agent and therefore believed the rest of Gert's stories.

When the next deportation order lay in our mailbox, Gert paid the Munich Gestapo another visit. "Call this phone number," he told them, "to receive your orders from my superiors." Once again, he enjoyed his success, his triumph over the Gestapo. When they found out who was on the other end of that phone number, they displayed a complete turnabout. "We are so sorry to have bothered you," they explained. "We didn't know that you serve in the S.D. Please give our apology to your family!"

Hey! How about that? An apology from the Gestapo! In Germany, the pecking order was always important. Gert had counted on that and he won!

27.   Dynamite

New Year's evening of 1944 was quite a memorable one. We knew all too well that the next few months were decisive, and if we could manage to survive until spring, we would have a new lease on life. The Allied Armies had taken Paris during the summer, and we had hoped that the war would end before Christmas; instead, the fighting went on and on along the Rhine, conditions were more terrible than ever, the cold and the lack of food was more and more threatening. Even the most convinced National Socialists were beginning to realize that they might have lost the war; but talk about miracle weapons was still heard; Gestapo measures were tightened as their security began to shake.

We knew on that last night of December that some desperate things were going to happen in case the entire structure of the Reich should soon begin to crumble. As the German army retreated, most prisoners of war and all political enemies of the system were afraid of mass executions as a last retribution. Just thinking of the near future was a depressing thing. We had several bottles of wine left from the past Christmas holiday gifts; and we exchanged them for a little food. The last one we kept for a toast to the New Year, but managed to drink only half a bottle between the three of us. We sat around reading, as we did so much of the time, and as the bells began to ring in 1945, we couldn't help but say; "Pretty soon we'll either make it for good, or we won't."

Actually, the end of the war turned out to be easier for us than we had expected. Hunger, sicknesses, bomb attacks, and the general confusion worked more in our favor than was expected. The first few days in May of 1945 saw a very unusual group of people assembled in our basement. There were two British soldiers who had escaped from a POW Camp, one German private, in civilian life an Austrian count and nephew of Count Stauffenberg (the convicted assassin of Adolf Hitler), and an SS officer who had been drafted as a reservist and decided that this was not his war and never had been. The four of them had been waiting for the end of hostilities for over four weeks in a tiny room in our basement.

At one time, this room was used as an auxiliary washroom, which means that it had a shower behind a curtain. We moved a heavy wooden shelf unit in front of its door in the hallway, and since it occupied a rather small area at the corner of the house, nobody would assume there was anything missing. There was another entrance to this refuge, a square area of bricks removed from the wall that bordered the large coal and wood storage room, and we kept this opening neatly covered with a huge wooden crate full of firewood. For supplies, visiting and occasional outings, we moved this box out of the way and crawled through the opening.

The four of them were prime examples of good behavior and amiable relationships. The two Germans had money to cover all expenses for the two POWs; time and again we had to warn all four of them, not to accompany their run-on card games with laughter that was too loud for comfort. They did not emerge from their hiding place until the entire German army had left the city, and a few days after the war was over, they had all gone in four different directions. I don't think they ever saw each other again afterwards.

The two British soldiers left the same day that the German army had reportedly withdrawn from the city; they asked if they could have our three bicycles until the American Third Army took over. My mother said that they could, but why three bicycles for the two of them? They wanted to pick up a fellow prisoner at the former camp; there was that problem of where the POW camp had been moved lately. We agreed to everything they said, but how was the third bicycle going to be taken along for the third man? My brother and the count had gone to explore the grounds of the nearby army base, to see if all the troops had really pulled out, and our SS officer refused to move from his hiding place in the basement; now that the war was this close to ending, he was not going to take the slightest chance whatsoever. After some discussion, I agreed to ride the bike halfway to their destination and make it back home on foot afterwards.

The streets were deserted and everything was in total darkness. The two men rode very fast, and I had great trouble keeping up with them. Now and then, one could hear the heavy artillery rumbles in the distance. All of a sudden, there was a series of shots nearby. I was so frightened that I fell off the bicycle, as did the two soldiers. They offered to walk the three bikes the rest of the way: I ran back home as fast as I could.

When I got back, my heart was pounding so hard that I thought it might burst. I felt sick the rest of the night, but we heard later that the two guys had picked up their friend and all three of them were taken in by the American field hospital after it had put up its huge tents on the lawns of Nymphenburg Castle; one of them had been wounded in the head.

At the evacuated German army base, my brother and the count ran into an old friend who was just leaving the premises with a small wagon loaded full of canned goods; he said that all the doors had been forcibly opened by mobs of people right after the army had retreated elsewhere, and the remaining supplies, foods and fuel, were carried off by all kinds of hungry people. This guy handed my brother two large cans from his overloaded little vehicle, and that was what we were going to have to eat that week. We saved the precious things until Sunday and when time came for dinner, my mother could not get the cans opened.

She was working on them furiously, driving the can opener down into the metal with a hammer, when I remarked that I certainly hoped it was worth all that trouble, since we didn't even know what was in them. "It looks like canned meat," we agreed because the cans were much larger than average household goods of fruit and vegetables. Being army supplies, they were not marked except for a very small sign on the bottom of each can.

"I can't get it open, whatever it is!" my mother said and continued hitting the thing with her hammer with all the determination that an approaching Sunday dinner can lend to a very hungry family.

In the meantime, my brother was staring glassy-eyed at the bottom of the other can. All of a sudden, he lunged over, ripped the hammer away from her, and sat down and wiped the sweat off his forehead. "You know what this is, people?" he asked quietly. Long silence. "I think it's dynamite, canned dynamite, that's what that is." There was no Sunday dinner, and we stayed as hungry as we were, also grateful, very grateful for what we didn't have that day.

Still very hungry, I decided to go exploring at the army base the next day. My brother was gone some place, my mother was home in bed, her favored refuge, and I was hungry. I picked up a large basket, some white paper, and walked all the way across the field and past the highway called Dachauerstrasse. There, the long row of buildings that was once an army base became visible and I joined several people who were probably looking for the same things that I was looking for: food.

Inside the big gate, a lot was going on. Everyone was carrying heavy loads, several guys were trying to move a small four-wheel cart piled high full of stuff. On one side I could see the railroad tracks with one boxcar still on them, doors broken off and all the contents of the car strewn all over the place.

As I came closer, I could see mounds of white-and-yellow powder right on the railroad tracks. Somebody told me that the boxcar had been full of them and that people had tried to carry off the sacks; when these proved to be too heavy for them, they emptied out half the sacks of flour, sugar, and rice where they stood in order to get away with the rest. I spread my paper on the bottom of the basket and filled it with the clean part of the goodies that were mounded on the tracks; but I was so scared to attract attention that I fled the scene in a hurry with just enough to last a couple of days.

On the way home, I gathered an armful of firewood that I found scattered around. When I started to cross the Dachauerstrasse once more, somebody shouted: "Look, here they are! Be careful! Run!" There was no choice for me: I could not let go of my heavy basket or the firewood, I was too tired to run. I crossed the big highway that came straight away from Dachau right in front of the first American tank.

This was history, and I saw it passing by, the end of the years of struggle for survival. This was the Third Army coming into the city after liberating the prisoners of the death camp at Dachau nearby. The soldiers looked grim and tense, not in any mood for friendly greeting. Slowly, tank after tank rolled by, the guns of each pointed in all directions. On top of some of the tanks, soldiers were covering the area

143

with their machine guns. If it hadn't been the day I had been waiting for, I would have been afraid.

After the tanks came the infantry, walking on both sides of the road, each man with a gun in hand, their eyes searching for danger. I pulled the large piece of white paper from under my foodstuff and waved it in slow half circles before my eyes. Not that anyone noticed it. There were no other people standing by the side of the road, most of them had walked away when they saw what was happening. I couldn't move. I kept on giving my sign of welcome, waving my piece of white paper. It seemed to me that one who knew what these troops had been through should give them some sign. Finally, tears were streaming down my face. The war had ended.

28.   The Tightrope Act Ends

Officially, the war ended on May 8th, 1945, but not for us. A few days after the Third Army had occupied the city, a jeep drove up in front of our place. Two American solders came in and arrested our mother. They took her away very quickly and did not say a word. Late that evening, after a strict curfew had emptied the city streets, two MPs and one of the arresting agents from early morning brought her back; he declared that they had made a mistake; it was my brother instead who was wanted by the CIC. The CIC agent spoke fluent German, and he revealed to us that Gert had been in Spain as a German spy.

I snarled at him: "You are making a second mistake! You are supposed to be our liberator." This agent of the American Secret Service seemed much too young for the job. "What do you mean?" I cried. "You have no idea what we have been through!" He turned toward me. He put his hand on my head, almost lovingly and said: "Don't worry; it will all come to light."

They kept my brother four whole days at the Mauerkirchner "Ritter von Epp Palais," where the CIC had made its headquarters. Gert told us after his return that he had to wait two days in the main hall, together with high-ranking Nazis, Gestapo and SS people. He said this was definitely humiliating.

Then came a long interview, more accurately an inter-rogation. They were well informed. Gert's entry visa for Spain was stamped by the German S.D. (secret service).

145

They knew that he had made contact with the British in Madrid. Gert's account of the twelve years of persecution was submitted to the other CIC officials; after another nerve-wracking day, he was set free.

On the following Sunday, the same day, the jeep parked in front of our place again, we had just begun to breathe a little easier. Were we about to endure the same cat-and-mouse-game with reversed prefix? I was beside myself. *It looks to me that stupidity is king,* I was thinking. *If there is a God, wouldn't he have to interfere right now?*

The American was alone this time. He introduced himself to Mother and to me: "My name is Lloyd, and I have something to discuss with Gert." The use of first names among complete strangers is not customary in Germany; only family members or very close friends call each other by their first name. Gert was out on his bicycle, looking for food, like most people. My mother said; "I can assure you, Officer, that he'll be back soon."

Lloyd explained that he was not an officer, but a civilian in the service of Army Intelligence. "We are facing difficult problems in a foreign country," he continued, "and we need the help of native Germans to sort things out."

"Has Gert been found trustworthy, I hope?" I asked with a twist of irony. I was furious and he noticed: "Here's a Care packet for you, you must be hungry." "No, thank you," I said, "I had something to eat last week; I am not such a big eater."

Lloyd gave the Care packet to Mother; she thanked him and offered him a taste of the famous Munich beer. It was a blazing hot day; and Lloyd admitted he was very thirsty. Mother sent me to bring a bottle from our small supply of beer in the basement. I took the Care package with me and ate an entire can of "Libby's Fruit Cocktail" in one sitting. Then I came back upstairs with a glass and opened the resealable bottle. German beer still came in bottles that could be resealed after opening. The American took a few big gulps and spit out the rest of it. He called the soldiers who were waiting in the jeep and told them to take him to the field hospital. He looked ashen and left without a word.

Closer inspection of the bottle revealed what had happened: it was filled with kerosene! How could such a thing happen? Apparently, somebody must have stored some kerosene in this resealable bottle. Our camp stove was fueled with kerosene. I had another sleepless night, because kerosene is toxic. I had never killed anybody, but this could be the first time. Is there no end to stupidity?

In the morning, I told Gert that I had waited for the day we would be free for about ten years, only to poison our "liberator" when he walks in! Gert was helpful, as usual: "I have the phone number of the office where he works. Call and ask for Lloyd Baysdorfer, who is probably sitting at his desk; at least you'll find out if he is sick and that would be better than doing nothing."

For several days I inquired if Mr. Baysdorfer had returned to work. No, he was still absent because of illness.

After what seemed to me to be an eternity, Lloyd answered the phone. "I am so glad you are back," I managed to explain; "Thank God I didn't kill you! It is by far the dumbest thing I have ever done! Can you believe that I didn't mean it?"

"You were worried about me?" asked Lloyd cheerfully. "The guys at my office have been teasing me about my success with the German fräulein who called here for me every day." There was a long silence and then he said, "It has been such a long time since anybody worried about me."

"Are you sure you are feeling all right?" I cried, "I am still worried sick!"

"If you make me a cup of tea this time," said Lloyd, to

my amazement, "I would like to tell you how many times this war has poisoned all of us."

"Please do that soon," I said. "I will be so very glad to see you well!"

Lloyd brought us another Care package. He told me that his stomach was pumped out and that the field hospital would not release him for days. "You can stop crying," he reassured me, "I feel perfectly fine, I seem to be used to being poisoned. It doesn't bother me at all." He was laughing, but I was not in the mood to laugh.

"You are too generous, Lloyd! I almost killed you, and I think you need to be more careful. Do you need somebody to taste your food and drink for you?" I couldn't believe he was smiling. "Okay with me, I accept your offer."

I was speechless, impressed by his generosity of spirit, also by his fluent, accent-free German. All of these young men, most of them not even twenty years old, those who were still alive after the invasion of Normandy, had actually gone to war to help us. Lloyd changed the subject; "I have this Care package for you, aren't you hungry?"

"No, thank you, I had something to eat last week; do you realize that you restored my faith in God, that you brought us a future free of fear?" I meant it, I embraced him.

"You need to come to the United States with me," he said quietly.

I don't like to end my history of the Hitler era with a war-time love story; but I have been truthful through all these pages, and that was how it ended for me in May of 1945, with a love story.

My mother and brother went to work immediately, together with the American Division for Information Control (ICD), rebuilding the cultural life of our largely destroyed city. They had no trouble rejoining the German "*Filmkammer*," whereas all former Nazis didn't get a chance.

Called to Berlin after the Second World War, Mother received the golden film award from the German Minister for the Interior, Friedrich Zimmermann.

After Mother and Gert had found their place in the peaceful economy of postwar Germany, Lloyd and I married in August of 1948. We made our home in the San Francisco Bay Area.